The Crisis of Western Philosophy

ESALEN INSTITUTE / LINDISFARNE PRESS
LIBRARY OF RUSSIAN PHILOSOPHY

The Meaning of Love, Vladimir Solovyov
War, Progress, and the End of History, Vladimir Solovyov
The Russian Idea, Nikolai Berdyaev
Sophia, The Wisdom of God, Sergius Bulgakov
Lectures on Divine Humanity, Vladimir Solovyov

THE CRISIS
of
WESTERN
PHILOSOPHY

(Against the Positivists)

VLADIMIR SOLOVYOV

Translated and Edited by Boris Jakim

LINDISFARNE PRESS

Translated from the Russian by Boris Jakim.

This edition copyright Lindisfarne Press 1996

Published by Lindisfarne Press
RR4 Box 94-A1, Hudson, N.Y. 12534

Library of Congress Cataloging-in-Publication Data

Solovyov, Vladimir Sergeyevich, 1853–1900.
  [Krizis zapadnoĭ filosofii, English.]
  The crisis of western philosophy : against the positivists /
Vladimir Solovyov ; translated by Boris Jakim.
      p.   cm. — (Esalen Institute/Lindisfarne Press Library of
Russian philosophy)
  Includes index.
  ISBN 0-940262-73-8 (paper)
  1. Positivism. 2. Solovyov, Vladimir Sergeyevich, 1853–1900.
I. Title. II. Series: Library of Russian philosophy.
B4263.K72E5 1996
146'.4—dc20   95-49263
                                                              CIP

Design & editorial services: Watersign Resources

10 9 8 7 6 5 4 3 2 1

Printed in the United States of America

Contents

Translator's Preface

Vladimir Solovyov (1853–1900) is coming to be seen as one of the seminal thinkers of the nineteenth century. After Dostoevsky and Tolstoy, he is the most gigantic figure of late nineteenth-century Russia. He can be considered the founder of modern Russian religious philosophy, and his work was one of the sources of the great blossoming of Russian literature and art that extended roughly from the mid-1890s to the 1920s and is called the "Silver Age." It may well be that Solovyov's unique synthetic vision of divine humanity and Christian politics will not be fully assimilated and acted upon until well into the twenty-first century.

The Crisis of Western Philosophy: Against the Positivists (1874) was the first in a series of works (also including *The Philosophical Principles of Integral Knowledge* (1877), *The Critique of Abstract Principles* (1877–80), and *Lectures on Divine Humanity* (1877–81)) in which Solovyov first developed his religious philosophy. In the *Crisis of Western Philosophy*, Solovyov undertook (as this work's subtitle indicates) a dense critique of positivism,[1] by which he meant the entire philosophy of Western rationalism from John Scotus Erigena onwards.

According to Aleksei Losev,[2] Solovyov distinguishes in the history of Western philosophy a succession of periods: (1) in which the authority of faith is dominant, (2) in which reason and faith hold equal sway, and (3) in which reason predominates over the authority of faith. For Solovyov these three periods are part of the past that has been overcome.

Solovyov finds repugnant in the modern period the individual reason's war against nature (akin to the earlier war of the individual reason against the authority of faith). Worst of all for Solovyov is the subordination of nature to reason in Western philosophy from Descartes to Hegel. Completely natural and necessary for Solovyov is the appearance of materialism as a reaction to the metaphysics of reason. But positivism, the leading philosophy in Solovyov's own time, is also bankrupt.

Solovyov believed, as Maxim Herman points out,[3] that only the philosophy of Schopenhauer and Eduard von Hartmann (1842–1906) could provide a way out of the impasse in which Western philosophy now found itself. By recognizing the error of the two great currents of Western philosophy, pure rationalism and pure empiricism, Hartmann had, according to Solovyov, established a true philosophical method. In place of the substances and abstract personifications of the former philosophy, Hartmann acknowledged an all-one, concrete spirit as the absolute principle. The sovereign good is achieved only by the whole ensemble of beings and only at the end of a universal evolution, whose goal is the suppression of the exclusive self-assertion of isolated beings and their restitution as realms of beings embraced by the universality of the absolute spirit.

Solovyov concludes[4] that Hartmann's philosophy affirms the same truths that are affirmed by the great theological doctrines of the ancient (and especially Christian) East. The tendency of this new philosophy is to unite the content of Eastern spiritual meditations with the logical perfection of Western form. The realization of this synthesis of science, philosophy, and religion should be the final goal of the intellectual evolution that will restore the unity of the realm of the spirit.

As Aleksei Losev puts it,[5] the main point of the *Crisis of Western Philosophy* is that "no preceding stage of philosophy can be ignored. Every preceding stage is one-sided and will find its appropriate place only when we are emancipated from Western philosophy in its entirety and surrender ourselves to the authority of faith." All the one-sided currents of Western philosophy— and their one-sidedness bears witness to the impotence of their striving toward absolute knowledge—can be understood only in the light of this authoritative faith.

The Crisis of Western Philosophy introduces Solovyov's great theme of total unity, which was to become perhaps the dominant theme of Russian philosophy. It is the work in which Solovyov first "became Solovyov," and in this sense it launched Russian religious philosophy, a philosophy developed by such major thinkers as Sergius Bulgakov, Pavel Florensky, Nikolai Berdyaev, and S. L. Frank.

NOTES TO THE PREFACE

1. Positivism was the dominant intellectual current in Russia in the 1870s, but, as Aleksei Losev points out (see his Russian book, *Vl. Solovyov*, 2d ed. [Moscow, 1994], p. 142), this decade also witnessed a reaction against positivism among academic philosophers. Two important public lectures against positivism were read in 1874: On January 12, the Moscow University professor and mathematician V. Ya. Zinger read a lecture entitled "The Exact Sciences and Positivism"; on October 1, the professor of the Moscow Religious Academy V. D. Kudriavtsev read a lecture entitled "Religion and Positive Philosophy." *The Crisis of Western Philosophy* is the most profound expression of this reaction against positivism.

2. Losev, pp. 143–44.
3. Maxim Herman, *Vladimir Soloviev: Sa vie et son oeuvre* (Paris, 1947), pp. 24–28.
4. Ibid.
5. Losev, p. 144.

TRANSLATOR'S ACKNOWLEDGEMENTS

I am grateful to Catherine Charuk for giving me permission to use portions of her manuscript translation of the Introduction to *The Crisis of Western Philosophy*.

I have also used Maxim Herman's excellent French translation (*Crise de la philosophie occidentale*, Paris, 1947) as an aid in interpreting some of the more obscure passages in the original.

Introduction

❖

This book is based on the conviction that philosophy in the sense of an abstract, *exclusively* theoretical knowledge has ended its development and passed irretrievably into the world of the past. This conviction differs from the usual negative attitude toward philosophy, the systematic expression of which we find in so-called *positivism*. It differs from positivism because, in the first place, it refers *both* to the *speculative* current of philosophy, what positivists call *metaphysics*, and to the *empirical* current, i.e., to that which finds its ultimate and fullest expression in positivism itself. Secondly, this conviction of mine differs from the positivist one because, although I recognize that the abstract-philosophical development has ended, I do not consider it fruitless. On the contrary, I recognize that it has led to certain positive results, the delineation of which is the principal task of this book. Thirdly, the self-satisfied certainty with which positivism draws, from the groundlessness of the old metaphysics, the conclusion that metaphysical questions are, in themselves, groundless and therefore must be abandoned completely—this certainty seems to me extremely limited and unjustified. I hope, on the contrary, to demonstrate that the concluded philosophical development has bequeathed to the very near future a complete and universal resolution of those questions, which were resolved one-sidedly and therefore unsatisfactorily in the course of that development. Finally, yet another essential difference between my view and the positivist view can be better clarified by an exposition of that philosophical development itself, to which I now turn.

Philosophy as a certain *rational* (reflective) knowledge is always a matter of *personal* reason. By contrast, in other spheres of common human activity, personal reason, the separate person, plays a more passive role: the *genus* acts. We find the same sort of *impersonal* activity here as in a beehive or an anthill. It is indeed certain that the basic elements in the life of humanity—*language*, *mythology*, and the primary forms of *society*—are, in their formation, completely independent of the *conscious will* of separate *persons*. For science in its present state, there is no doubt that neither language nor the political state is produced by the conscious activity of individuals. They are not invented by separate persons, just as, for example, the structure of a beehive is not invented by individual bees. Neither can *religion* in the proper sense of the word (where it is not mythology) be invented. In religion too the individual as such has only a passive significance, insofar as an external revelation independent of human beings is recognized as the *objective* source of religion, and insofar as the faith of national masses, determined by a common tradition, and not the inquiry of personal reason, is the *subjective* basis of religion. Turning, finally, to *artistic creativity*, we find that, although its subject is undoubtedly the person of the artist,[1] for true art it is necessary that the artists not remain in their clear and separate consciousness, but transcend it in ecstatic inspiration. Hence, the less personal reflection there is in a work of art, the greater will be its artistic worth. By contrast, *philosophical knowledge* is expressly an activity of the personal reason or the separate person in all the clarity of this person's individual consciousness. The subject of philosophy is preeminently the singular *I* as a knower. (Of course, this definition is only relative, like all others.)

Philosophy is therefore a world-view of *separate* individuals. The common world-view of *nations* and tribes always has a *religious*, not a philosophical, character. Therefore, as long as *all* separate individuals live by the common spiritual life of the nation, philosophy as an independent and sovereign world-view is impossible. The intellectual activity of individuals is wholly determined by national beliefs. This is clear *a priori* and is historically unquestionable. Thus, philosophy arises only when, for thinking individuals, the faith of the nation ceases to be their own faith, loses for them the significance of an inner unconscious conviction, and, instead of a principle of life, becomes merely an object of thought. Philosophy begins when thinking individuals separate their thought from the common faith, oppose it to this faith as to something *external*.

In the Middle Ages the common life of the Western nations was entirely determined by a certain religious world-view, namely by Christianity in the form which it received in the Roman Catholic Church. Philosophy in the West could begin then only when for certain individuals the teaching of the Catholic Church ceased to correspond to their own thought and therefore ceased to be their inner conviction. Instead, this teaching became for them an external authority. Western philosophy begins with a split between individual thought as reason and the common national faith as authority (*ratio et auctoritas*). This relationship between knowledge and faith, reason and authority, has a fundamental, determining significance for medieval philosophy, or *scholasticism*. The logical and historical development of this relationship passed through the following three main stages or moments:

1. The Christian teaching that is affirmed by the Catholic Church to be divine revelation is the absolute *truth*. But my personal thought does *not correspond* to this teaching; my *reason* is not in accord with it. *Ergo*: My thought is in error, and my reason is false. Postulate: It is necessary to subordinate reason to authority, to renounce independent thought.

2. But if my thought is *rational*, it cannot contradict the *truth*. Thus, if the teaching of the Church is true, it must be in accord with my rational thought. "For true authority does not contradict right reason, nor does right reason contradict true authority, since both indubitably flow from a single source, i.e., divine wisdom."[2] Postulate: It is necessary to remove the contradiction of reason and authority, to *reconcile* the two.

3. But this reconciliation actually turns out to be the acknowledgment of the exclusive rights of reason, and the apparent condition "right reason does not contradict true authority" actually confers an absolute significance upon reason. In fact, reason does not contradict true authority, but what authority is true? That authority which does not contradict reason: "true authority does not contradict right reason." Thus, reason nevertheless has the decisive significance: it determines even its own *rectitudo* as well as *veritas auctoritatis*. On the other hand, in and of itself, authority does not yet have meaning; it can be false. Authority becomes meaningful only insofar as it is true, and its truth is determined by whether it is in accord with reason. Thus, only reason is true, and authority loses all significance. If authority is in accord with reason, it is obviously *not necessary*. If it contradicts reason, it is *false*. Therefore, at the end of the development one gets the same duality of reason and authority as at the first moment, but now in an inverse relation. Reason now has absolute significance, whereas authority, insofar

as it differs from reason, is seen to be false. This logically necessary conclusion became a widespread conviction of the Western intelligentsia only at the end of the Middle Ages. But powerful and consistent intellects clearly conceived and expressed it at the very beginning of scholasticism. Thus, John Scotus Erigena, to whom the words cited above belong, and who lived in the ninth century at the time of Charles the Bald, expresses with especial power and directness the absolute autocracy of reason and the utter impotence of any authority before reason. In his work *De divisione naturae*, written in the form of a dialogue between a teacher and his pupil, one finds the following discussion:

> *Master*: It is not unknown to you, I suppose, that what is first in nature has a greater dignity than what is first in time. *Disciple*: That is known to almost everyone. *Master*: We have been taught that reason is first in nature, while authority is first in time.[3]

But, in essence, authority does not even have this advantage:

> Even though nature was created together with time, still not from the beginning of time and nature was there authority. Together with nature and time, reason arose from the principle of things. *Disciple*: Reason itself teaches this. Authority arises from true reason, whereas reason never arises from authority. For any authority that is not approved by true reason turns out to be impotent. But true reason, indestructible and immutable thanks to its own powers, does not need any support from authority. It also appears to me that true authority is nothing other than truth found by the power of reason and handed down in a written form by the holy fathers to instruct later generations. Or perhaps you think differently? *Master*: By no means. Thus, in order to solve the problems that are before us, we must first turn to reason, and only then to authority.[4]

John Erigena's rationalism was not without followers. The monk Otlon, who lived in the eleventh century, said that he knew many dialecticians who attached such an importance to their science that they used it to limit the significance of the Holy Scripture and were greater followers of Boethius than of the Bible.[5] An especially influential representative of the rationalist current (although not as staunch a representative as Erigena) was the famous Abelard (1079–1142), who asserted that all that was essential in Christianity had already been known to the ancient philosophers since it was based on reason. Of interest is Abelard's work *Sic et Non* (*Yes and No*), in which, first protecting himself by a few pious remarks, he attempts to demonstrate the inner groundlessness of authority as it is expressed in the Holy Scripture and the teaching of the Fathers. If Erigena demanded of authority that it be in agreement with reason, Abelard, citing the Bible and the patristic writings at length, attempted to demonstrate that authority does not agree even with itself on all questions, important and unimportant. Therefore, before reconciling authority with reason, it is first necessary to reconcile it with itself and, evidently, this can be done only by reason. The internal contradiction of authority elicits *doubt*; doubt stimulates *inquiry*; inquiry reveals *truth* (*dubitando enim ad inquisitionem venimus, inquirendo veritatem percipimus*).[6]

But if truth is known through inquiry, the question naturally arises: Why is authority necessary? And here we indeed see that, toward the end of the Middle Ages, philosophical minds, instead of reconciling reason with faith, Aristotle with the Bible, like the earlier scholastics, wholeheartedly go over to the side of the reborn classical philosophy. Identifying this philosophy with reason, they directly acknowledge the contradiction between reason and religious authority, between philosophical truth and religious dogma as real and irreconcilable. For philosophers this is tantamount to the rejection of religious dogma.[7]

As regards the *content* of scholastic philosophy, the famous dispute between *realism* and *nominalism* is of some interest here.

The principle of realism was *universalia sunt ante rem* (the *universal*, i.e., the concept, *before the thing*, i.e., the particular), so that genuine reality was attributed only to general concepts. According to the definition of Thomas Aquinas, the absolute entity is an absolutely simple *form*, pure actuality without any potentiality. The principle of nominalism was the opposite one: *universalia post rem* (*the universal after the thing*). This principle negated the actual existence in things of that general content which is known in rational concepts. All of this general content was asserted by nominalism as being exclusively the product of the abstracting reason. The final conclusion was: *universalia sunt nomina*. Actuality belongs only to an individual thing, precisely only *as individual—haec res*. And since all knowledge is universal, it follows that true knowledge is impossible. This skeptical nominalism of Occam and his school rejected in this manner all resolution of the higher metaphysical questions, leaving them exclusively to *faith*, but without indicating any grounds for faith, which logically led to the *negation* of faith.

When the previous main object of reason—historical Christianity as an authority—was rejected, the immediate nature of things, the existing world, became the sole object of reason. A dualism lies at the beginning of modern philosophy as well, this time not between reason and faith, but between reason and nature, the external world, the object of reason. Reason, asserted as an independent principle in medieval philosophy, necessarily had to be victorious over authority. At the very beginning of the conflict, confidence in this victory had already been expressed by John Scotus Erigena, the first medieval thinker. On the other hand, in modern philosophy, reason, as an independent principle, had to engulf its object—i.e., the external world, nature—to liken this object to itself. Confidence in the dominance of reason over the external object was already clearly expressed by *Descartes*, the first representative of modern philosophy. Just as for Erigena authority becomes meaningful only when it is confirmed by reason (which, by contrast, does not require any confirmation from authority), so for Descartes the external world can be recognized as having genuine reality only when such reality is demanded by reason. The truth of reason here does not depend on any external confirmation; rather, reason itself contains within itself the whole basis of its truth—*cogito ergo sum* ("I think, therefore I am"). Although, in scholasticism, the autocracy of reason was proclaimed at the very beginning, this autocracy could not immediately attain universal recognition, but had to battle long against the external authority of Church teaching. In modern philosophy, on the other hand, the idea that nature was a being absolutely external to reason did not quickly yield to logical thought. And we see in England and France an entire school of so-called empirical philosophy, which asserts the complete subordination of rational knowledge to external experience. The conflict between reason and authority in scholasticism ended with the total victory of reason, a victory that left far behind it even the daring doctrine of John Erigena, who had asserted only the autonomy of reason and its primacy over authority. Now, at the close of medieval philosophy, the authority of Christian teaching was already beginning to be rejected as irrational. At the end of the development of modern philosophy, we see a just-as-theoretically-complete victory of reason over external immediate being, which now is not only subordinate to reason, as in Descartes, but is directly negated as meaningless in Fichte and Hegel. Such is the analogy between scholasticism and modern philosophy (up to and including Hegel). The essence of both is the conflict of autonomous reason, of the thinking *I*, with a principle external to it: in scholasticism, with the external authority of the Church, with historical externality; in modern philosophy, with the external being of nature, with physical externality. The course of our inquiry now brings us to an examination of the main aspects or moments of this second conflict.

At the basis of Descartes' philosophy lies the following criterion for the truth of our knowledge: "All things that we *conceive* clearly and distinctly are true according to the manner in which we conceive them." Therefore, "the things that one conceives clearly and distinctly to be different substances truly are different substances."[8] "From the fact alone," Descartes says further, "that I can draw from my thought the idea of a certain thing, it follows that everything that I know clearly and distinctly as belonging to that thing belongs to it in fact."[9] On the basis of this criterion Descartes asserts: "However, on the one hand, I have a clear and distinct idea of myself insofar as I am a thinking thing but without extension, and on the other hand I have a distinct idea of my body insofar as it is only an extended but not a thinking thing. In view of this, it is certain that I, i.e., my soul, by which I am what I am, is entirely and truly distinct from my body."[10] Therefore, two kinds of things or substances independent of one another must necessarily be admitted: a thinking substance (*res cogitans*) and an *extended* or *bodily* substance (*res extensa*), since extension in three dimensions constitutes the whole genuine nature of a body (because it is known clearly and distinctly), while thinking (for the same reason) constitutes the whole genuine nature of a spirit. For all else that can be attributed to a body presupposes extension and is only a certain quality or modification (*modus*) of an extended thing, just as all that we find in a spirit consists only in different modifications of thinking.[11] Descartes thus reduces the whole content of the external world to formal mathematical definitions of extension, to spatial relationships. He excludes any living force from nature. (It is well known that he considered even animals to be only complex machines without their own life.) The only movement he admits is mechanical movement caused by external impact. In the same way, he reduces the whole content of the human spirit to the formal activity of thinking, by which he means, in general, representation. For Descartes, will is only an *accidens* of thinking, in essence nothing other than judgment ("acts of will, i.e., judgments").[12]

Thus, the essential content of all that exists is only thinking and that which is accessible to clear and analytical, i.e., rational, thinking in external nature—extension. Nevertheless, Descartes admits the actual multiplicity of separate things or substances, to which thinking and extension belong as their essential attributes. He admits the genuine existence of a multiplicity of bodies and a multiplicity of spirits. But what conditions this multiplicity, what differentiates substances from one another? Let us first take heterogeneous substances: How does a given extended substance differ from a given thinking substance? According to Descartes' definition, presented above, the difference lies in the fact that the extended substance is *only* extended and does not think, whereas the thinking substance *only* thinks and is not extended. That is, the whole difference consists only in the *attributes* of extension and thinking, not in the *substances* themselves as such, for both are equally substances and, as such, do not differ from one other. Further: How do *homogeneous* substances differ from one another? How does one extended thing, for example, differ from another? Since the whole content of an extended substance consists, according to Descartes, in extension, one extended substance can differ from another only in *particular* forms or *modifications* of extension. In fact, one material object is distinguished or separated from another by its position in space, by its size, shape, relation of parts, etc. All these are only particular modifications of extension and have no connection with the substance itself. One must also speak of the interrelationship of two thinking substances, insofar as thinking and its particular forms have the same relation to a thinking substance as extension with its particular forms has to an extended substance. But if every distinction or separation therefore consists in attributes and their modifications (modes), and by no means in the substances themselves, if the substances themselves, *as substances*, do not differ from one another in any way, if they are absolutely identical, then it is clear that *many* substances do not exist. Rather, there is only *one* substance, and thinking and extension are equally its attributes. But, in this case, what are separate, individual entities and things? In their separateness they cannot be substances, for substance is one. Nor can they be its attributes, for an attribute, according to its very concept, is the common content of all homogeneous things. It remains but to recognize individual things as particular modifications or *modes* of attributes. A separate material object will be a *mode of extension*, while a separate thinking entity or spirit will be a *mode of thinking*.

Thus, logically developing Descartes' principles, we get the complete formula of Spinozism: "By substance I understand that which is in itself and is understood through itself, i.e., that, the concept of which does not need the concept of another thing for its formation."[13] This is the most general definition of that which absolutely is, and in this sense substance is accepted by all points of view, not excluding materialism with its independent matter and positivism with its "unknowable" absolute. From this definition it follows, first of all, that substance is infinite in all respects, for if it were limited in any respect, it would be determined here by *another*, which contradicts its concept. Secondly, it follows that substance, containing all actuality, can be only one, and this one infinite substance Spinoza calls God or *active nature* (*natura naturans*).

"By attribute I understand that which a mind knows in substance, as composing its essence."[14] The essential content or attributes of substance determine for us thinking and extension, which are only two aspects of one and the same thing, and cannot be separated from one another.

"By mode I understand the state of substance or that which is in another, through which it is understood."[15] All individual or particular entities and things are such modifications or states of substance according to its two attributes: "Particular things are nothing but states of God's attributes or modes by which God's attributes are expressed in a certain determinate manner."[16] Because of the substantial unity of the attributes their separate modifications are correspondingly identical, so that every existence is, on the one hand, a mode of extension, i.e., a certain body, and, on the other hand, a mode of thinking, i.e., a certain idea. And these two modes are one and the same thing, but expressed in two ways.[17] Therefore, "The order and connection of an idea are the same as the order and connection of things."[18]

Substance is the sole absolute existent in itself, *causa sui*. The multiplicity of finite being originates from substance and exists only in substance, as its modifications. It originates from it and exists in it *necessarily*, for, since outside of substance there is nothing, all that is produced by substance follows from the proper inner nature of substance and is therefore absolutely necessary. But it is clear that this far from completes the task of philosophy. One must still show *what* constitutes the necessity for substance to produce the finite world. One must show *in what manner* the manifestation of substance in the multiplicity of separate existences, in *natura naturata*, necessarily follows from its inner nature. Spinoza dogmatically asserts that an infinite number of modes eternally proceed from the infinite nature of substance in an infinite manner with the same necessity as it eternally follows from the nature of a triangle that the sum of its angles equals two right angles.[19] However, this assertion already *presupposes* multiple being as given, but does not *explain* it. Indeed, if one directly recognizes the existence of finite things as a given fact, it is certain that these finite things, by definition having no being in themselves, must be posited by substance.

And since, by the very concept of substance, there cannot be anything accidental in it, these finite things must follow from the very nature of substance in an absolutely necessary manner, and, moreover, in an infinite number, since one cannot conceive a limited number in substance. This is how it *must be* if one is to presuppose a given multiplicity of finite things. But in philosophy, by its essence, a given reality is precisely that which must be explained or derived—a problem to be solved. It is by no means a presupposition. However, only that which contains its proper necessity in itself can be an absolute presupposition, an absolute *prius*, in philosophical explanation or derivation. Such in Spinoza is the concept of substance. "Substance," he says, "by nature, precedes its states."[20] In itself, in abstraction from its modes ("testimony of states and considered in itself"),[21] substance already fully possesses existence by virtue of its nature or essence, since it is "the cause of itself, whose essence includes existence."[22] If this is the case, in what then does the necessity of finite things consist? Where does *number*, even if infinite, in substance come from? Where does the multiplicity in it come from? Clearly, multiple and finite being does not follow from the nature of substance. And if Spinoza asserts the contrary, it is only because he finds this being in empirical reality. If he had strictly adhered to his principle, Spinoza would have had to argue in the following manner: The only thing that truly is, is substance. Since, by its very concept, substance is absolute reality in itself, it does not contain the necessity of anything else, and it therefore does not contain the necessity of finite things as its modes. That is, finite things do not exist necessarily, and since nothing can exist by accident, finite things do not exist at all. Spinoza's principle therefore logically leads not to the explanation but to the negation of the given reality. This clearly shows the deficiency of this principle, despite all the indisputable truth it contains. This deficiency was implicitly recognized by Spinoza himself, for, while denying all multiplicity in the abstract unity of substance, at the same time he affirmed this multiplicity, supposedly necessarily following from substance. This contradiction removes the one-sidedness of the system, conditioning the transition to the opposite principle. In fact, the assertion that the multiplicity of modes is necessarily and eternally posited by substance is equivalent to the assertion that substance is necessarily and eternally manifested in finite things, and thus does not exist by itself without this manifestation. Substance in its abstraction is only a potentiality, a pure possibility, which is actualized only in the multiplicity of finite being. Not having its own existence apart from finite phenomena, substance is only unity in their multiplicity, i.e., the necessary order common to them, the eternal link connecting them, the law of cosmic harmony, and so on.

In this manner all reality has once again gone over to the side of individual things. But this is not a mere return to the separate thinking and extended substances of Descartes. Spinoza removed this abstract duality by admitting the substantial identity of thinking and extension, soul and body. The soul for Spinoza is only the idea of the body, or the body in ideal act, while the body is the soul as object, or extended idea. Therefore, there is no soul without a body, but there is also no body without a soul. All of bodily nature, all individual things are animated ("All individuals are animate, although to different degrees").[23] This is an important step beyond Descartes, who denied the animateness even in animals and separated the human spirit by an impassable chasm not only from the rest of nature but also from its own body. However, the substantial identity of soul and body in Spinoza remains wholly abstract. Nothing determinate can be understood by it as long as the essence of bodily or material being is posited in extension, for extension *in abstracto*, i.e., a thing that is *only* extended (as understood by Descartes and

Spinoza), has nothing in common with thinking. The actual synthesis of the concepts of soul and body was achieved by Leibniz with his principle of the monad, which resulted from a transformation of the concept of bodily substance:

> If the essence of bodies consisted in extension, this extension alone should be sufficient to explain all of their properties. But that is not the case. We remark in matter a quality by which bodies resist movement in some manner, so that it is necessary to employ a force to move them.[24]

Leibniz continues:

> This lets us know that there is in matter something other than that which is purely geometric, i.e., other than extension and its simple change. On closer inspection, we perceive that it is necessary to introduce some superior or metaphysical notion, namely, the notion of substance, action, and force; these notions imply that anything that is passive must act reciprocally, and anything that acts must experience some reaction. I am in agreement that all bodies, by nature, are extended, and that there is no extension without a body. However, one should not confuse the notions of place, space, or pure extension with the notion of substance, which, aside from extension, also includes resistance, i.e., action and passion.[25]

Descartes' main error, according to Leibniz, consists in the meaningless identification of extension with bodily substance, as a result of a misunderstanding of the nature of substance in general.[26] Leibniz says:

> The idea of force or potential, called *Kraft* by the Germans and force by the French, sheds much light on the true concept of substance. Active force differs from the pure potential of the scholastics in that the this pure potential is only an imminent possibility of action, requiring an external stimulus for its transition to real action, whereas an active force contains a certain kind of act or entelechy, which

occupies the middle ground between the ability to act and the action itself. An active force presupposes an effort and therefore enters into activity (*operatio*) by itself (*per se*), having no need for assistance (coaction) from outside.[27]

Thus, I say that this active property belongs to every substance, that from this there always proceeds a certain action, and that, consequently, bodily substance itself, just like spiritual substance, never stops acting.[28]

Matter is represented as consisting of atoms or actual units, but these elements of matter themselves cannot be material, for matter, being divisible to infinity, i.e., completely passive, does not contain the principle of actual unity. An actual atom presupposes resistance to division, i.e., action out of itself. It is an independent force, "and from this there follows something analogous to sensation and desire, so that it is necessary to understand these active forces or monads by analogy with the concept that we have of the soul."[29]

A monad is a force that is constantly acting and, therefore, constantly changing. According to the concept of the monad as a spontaneous force, these changes proceed from an internal principle. But besides *the principle of change*, there is necessarily presupposed in the monad a *determination* of that which changes, a determination that would constitute the *peculiarity* of monads and condition their *diversity*. For, in the contrary case, all monads, not differing from one another in any way, would constitute a single entity according to Leibniz's law of the identity of the undifferentiables—*principium identatis indiscernibilium*—and the actual multiplicity of that which exists would thus be impossible:[30]

This determination must contain multiplicity in a unit or in that which is simple, for any natural change occurs gradually; something changes and something remains, and it is therefore necessary that a simple substance contain a multiplicity of states and relationships, although it has no parts.

> A transient state containing and forming a multiplici-
> ty in a unity or a simple substance is nothing but that
> which is called a representation (*perceptio*).
>   The action of the internal principle (in the monad) pro-
> ducing the change or the transition from one representation
> to another can be called a striving or desiring (*appetitio*).[31]

Thus, the basic elements of all that exists, simple substances, are monads. A monad is an active force (*vis activa*), its
action being determined as representation and striving. All that
exists is thus not only animate but even consists of souls. In
Descartes, objective reality has the form of an extended thing
absolutely different and separate from the thinking subject.
Spinoza then considered objective reality to be identical with
thinking in a single substance and indissolubly linked with
thinking in this substance's modes. In Leibniz, this objective
reality, material being, loses its independence from the thinking
subject, because the subjective activity of representation and
striving is acknowledged as the basis of objective being, and the
nonmaterial monad is seen as the substance of the *material*
body. Even though all substantiality has thus gone over to the
subjective or psychic side, this does not eliminate the complete
externality between the knower and that which is known. In
effect, Leibniz confers the significance of substances upon separate psychic units and considers them to be fully independent
entities, which produce the entire content of their representation out of themselves. But if that is the case, every monad as a
knowing subject has the totality of other monads absolutely
outside of itself, without any possibility of any actual relationship whatever. I—a given monad—produce the whole world
represented by me out of myself. This is only my representation, but the actual independent world outside of me corresponds to this subjective representation. Such a
correspondence is presupposed by Leibniz, but to explain it he
uses only expressions that do not have logical content. Thus, he

speaks of the pre-established harmony between the subjective representations of each monad and the reality of the world external to it. Further, he speaks of the fact that each monad is a mirror, as it were, which more or less clearly reflects the whole world. To this are related very profound hints at the perfect correspondence between the physical and moral worlds (the kingdom of nature and the kingdom of grace), at the compatibility between mechanistic necessity and teleology, and so forth. While Leibniz's philosophy expresses forcefully and with full logical clarity the moment of multiplicity and independence of separate particular being, it presents for the opposite moment of general substance and unity only brilliant conjectures and clever metaphors, which belong to the philosopher personally but have not become part of the general trove of philosophical ideas. Thus, on the one hand, a positive result of the philosophical development in Leibniz was the affirmation of the exclusive independence and primordiality of psychic, or subjective, being. On the other hand, the genuineness of knowledge as referring to that which actually exists and not merely expressing particular representations of each separate subject remained an undecided question. In other words, although the independence and reality of knowledge as a psychic act of separate monads were affirmed, its universal significance and objective unity remained doubtful. Modern philosophy reached the same dual result, i.e., an idealistic affirmation and a skeptical question, from another direction, namely in the English empirical school, which had its origin in Bacon and reached its extreme expression in David Hume and his latest followers.

Bacon is important only as the founder of the empirical current in modern philosophy. The positive content of his views does not have a philosophical character; it does not transcend the vulgar view for which the world represented by us has absolute reality with all the multiplicity of its objective content, exists by itself, outside of us, but at the same time can be known adequately by us. To achieve such adequate knowledge it is sufficient, in Bacon's opinion, to free the mind from deceitful presuppositions or prejudices (*idola*), as well as from the barren formalism of scholasticism, which imparts no real knowledge.

Vulgar realism receives a more drastic expression in Hobbes, who attributes existence exclusively to external, bodily being. This external being contains all reality; except for bodies, nothing exists. But this necessarily raises the question of the relation of the knowing subject to this external reality. The resolution of this question of knowledge is the task Locke sets for himself in his *Essay Concerning Human Understanding*.

Locke's philosophy is interesting because it twists objective realism, which appeared in Bacon and Hobbes with almost primitive immediacy, into its opposite—subjective idealism. Locke's point of departure is given by his predecessors: in their empiricism, the independent significance of the subject in knowledge is already denied implicitly. Locke places this denial at the basis of his philosophy, developing it in detail in his refutations of the theory of innate ideas. From the nonexistence of innate ideas, he draws the general conclusion that the knowing subject—our soul in itself—is something completely passive and contentless without external stimulation: a *tabula rasa*. We receive all of our knowledge from experience. First of all, we perceive through our senses the actions of external objects, which produce in us a series of representations referring to the external world. Secondly, observing or reflecting the inner states and actions that are stimulated in us by external experience, we receive another series of representations, which refer directly to our own psychic being. The source of our knowledge is therefore a two-fold experience: an external experience consisting of sensations and an inner experience consisting of psychic observations (reflection). But this division turns out to be only relative, for the data of external experience, i.e., those representations of ours which we refer to external objects, originate not directly from these objects (as certain ancient philosophers childishly believed) but from our own sensations, i.e., from changes in our sensuous state originating from the action of external objects. Thus, we know not the external objects themselves but only *our subjective* states, which can serve only as signs of external being. Like Descartes, Locke stopped midway, having divided our representations that refer to the external world into two categories: one (the so-called primary qualities, i.e., size, shape, position, number, motion) he considered to be objective reality, whereas he attributed to the second category (that of the derivative or "secondary qualities," i.e., color, sound, etc.) the exclusively subjective significance of sensations. But such a division is completely arbitrary. Once Locke rejected innate ideas, representations of size, shape, etc. could originate only from a combination of sensations, and they actually do originate from such a combination of visual and tactile sensations. Therefore, they have a significance that is just as subjective as that of any other of our representations, although they differ from them in other respects. Thus, the *whole* content of the external world has a subjective character, and external being is only the unknown cause of our sensations. But if that is the case, we do not have the right to attribute to this unknown cause material, objective being, because all that is material and objective is reduced to certain subjective elements. It is our representation, and not an existent in itself. A thing is not an existent, and an existent is not a thing. Thus, all material objects of the external world are only our representations or ideas. Therefore, the external world which consists of these objects does not, as such, have any being outside of our representation. This is Berkeley's fundamental principle.

Berkeley states:

> Everyone acknowledges that neither our thoughts nor our feelings nor our fantasies exist outside of their subject (the spirit). But it seems no less clear that different sensations and representations, however they may be blended or linked together (i.e., whatever objects they may form), cannot exist otherwise than in a spirit that represents them. This, I think, will be clear to anyone who directs his attention at the meaning of the expression "to exist" as it is applied to sensuous things. When I say that the table at which I am writing exists, this means that I see and touch it. If I were outside of my study I could affirm the existence of this table in the sense that, if I were there, I could touch it, or that some other subject is now touching it. That is the only rational meaning of this expression and similar expressions. For that which is usually said about the absolute existence of unthinking things, without any reference to their representability, turns out to be completely meaningless. The being (*esse*) of such things is their representability (*percipi*). It is not possible that they could have any existence outside of the spirits or thinking entities that represent them.[32]

If all material objects are only representations or ideas, it follows that they do not have any independence or proper activity. They are completely passive; their existence is wholly conditioned by another, i.e., by the spirit. Since by nature they are deprived of any active principle, they cannot act upon one another, or be the cause of one another. The activity that evokes ideas belongs exclusively to the spirit. Moreover, some of our representations are evoked by the activity of our own spirit. These are our thoughts and fantasies, or ideas in the narrow sense. But other representations appear in our consciousness independently of us; these are those which are formed out of sensations and constitute what are usually called things or external objects. Since these things are not produced by our own activity and are completely independent of our will, it is necessary to recognize that they are evoked in us by the action of another will not our own, the action of another spirit. These objective representations or objects differ from our subjective ideas by a greater force, clarity, determinateness, and constancy. Moreover, they find themselves in a certain regular connection with one another. That is, they are in a certain determinate order, as if according to certain rules called the laws of nature.[33] From these and other properties belonging to objective representations, we conclude that that other spirit which produces them in us is not a limited spirit like ours but is an infinite, or absolute, spirit.[34]

Thus, external material being loses here all its independence, being recognized as only a representation. But it retains its objective significance for the knower, thanks to its cause that is external to the knower—in the absolute spirit. While denying the causal connection between separate objects or representations and saying that the connection of representations does not include the relation of cause and effect,[35] Berkeley, does admit, however, a causal connection between the spirit and representations. He recognizes the spirit as the generating cause of representations, and in the case of objective representations he recognizes the absolute spirit as such a cause. Thus, for Berkeley, the world of the knowing subject is united with its external absolute principle only by the thin thread of the law of causality. When David Hume broke this thread, the regularity of the objective world was transformed into a random sequence of unconnected representations, and that which truly is was recognized as the absolutely unknown, as the pure X.

All we know, says Hume, is either our impressions and sensations or their reproduction in imagination and thought.[36] All our representations are united among one another in three ways: by *similarity*, *correlation in space and time*, and *causality*.[37]

But these relationships do not have any absolute significance; they do not express any inner necessary connection in things themselves. Although such a connection is usually seen in causality, yet, attentively analyzing any case of causal relationship, we will find in it only the fact that a certain phenomenon constantly follows another. Because we are accustomed to such a constant union, these phenomena appear to us as inseparably connected to each other.

This result of modern philosophy, negating all metaphysics as impossible, apparently confirms the view of positivism. It is true that, after Hume and partly out of his teaching, a new philosophical development arose beginning with Kant. It is important to find out to what extent the results of this philosophical development are favorable for positivism: to find out if their significance for philosophy is as purely negative as the results of the pre-Kantian metaphysics.

Chapter I

Astonishing and unexpected events are occurring in the intellectual history of our time, no less than in its political history. Was it long ago that it seemed totally certain that, after a long series of philosophical doctrines, each of which asserted itself as the absolute truth but was then refuted by the following doctrine as an error, the human mind (represented by Western thinkers) had finally found a haven in the negative result of positivism, which considered the resolution of the higher questions of thought to be absolutely impossible and their very posing absurd? But, at the present time, when this positive view has become so dominant that the word "metaphysics" has begun to be used only in a sense of absolute censure, as equivalent to nonsense, a new metaphysical system appears. In this system, these higher questions, rejected by positivism, are not only posed again but are resolved with unusual daring, sometimes reaching the fantastic. And this new metaphysics, instead of being ridiculed, as one might expect, achieves enormous, unprecedented success everywhere. It is embraced avidly; not only followers, but ecstatic adepts appear. Only the extreme, intellectually compelling force of the higher metaphysical questions can explain this phenomenon.

It follows that the matter is not so simple as the positivists think. It follows that it is insufficient to set aside the essential problems of thought, and that, instead, they must be solved at any cost. In view of this, the recent new attempt to solve them acquires a great importance. I am speaking of Eduard Hartmann's "philosophy of the unconscious." But since Hartmann himself links his doctrine with the preceding philosophical systems, seeing himself as their culminator, we must, in order to define his philosophical significance, recall the general course of Western philosophy beginning with Kant. We must do this because all philosophy after Kant is intimately connected with the revolution produced by his *Critique of Pure Reason.*

As is well known, the basic question that Kant's philosophy poses for itself is the question of knowledge. What is knowledge? Is it possible, and how is it possible, to know what actually is? Pre-Kantian metaphysics did not concern itself with this question. It took what it knew (the essence of things, etc.) as an object given independently of the knower, and did not investigate the possibilities of metaphysical knowledge. This character of philosophy, usually called dogmatism, was expressed with particular clarity in Wolff's system, which was dominant just before Kant. Admitting the existence of an objective world completely independent of and external to the knowing subject, this system asserted that we know this objective world (in ontology, rational cosmology, and psychology) by means of reason, that we know it in its essence, as it is in itself. And the organ of knowledge consists of the ideas and laws of thought innate to our reason. But how can the subject essentially know that which is outside of it and independent of it, and, in part, even essentially differs from it (such is the material substance assumed by Wolff)? This question was never posed. This was an unconscious metaphysics. "The human mind surrendered itself to metaphysical reveries as if in sleep, not giving and not asking for an accounting of their possibility." From this dogmatic reverie it was awakened by Kant.

As is well known, the shock that awakened Kant himself was David Hume's skepticism, which took all objective significance away from the fundamental rational law of causality, which derived this law from the accident of habit and thus made all certain knowledge, all science, impossible. Wishing to rescue science, Kant undertook an inquiry not only into the law of causality but also into all the other general forms of our knowledge. The result of this inquiry was two-fold: First, Hume's skepticism was refuted, for it was proved that the forms of our knowledge, being *a priori*, i.e., prior to any experience, have, as such, an apodictic certainty and a universal significance. Secondly, the dogmatic metaphysics was also destroyed, since it was recognized that all these forms of knowledge—both immediately sensuous knowledge (space and time) and rational knowledge (categories)—are precisely, in consequence of their *a priori* character, only general and necessary forms or laws of *our* knowledge, necessary conditions for *our* experience. By no means do these forms belong—as was supposed by dogmatism, which took them to be *veritates aeternae*—to the genuine nature of the world which exists outside of us and independently of us. By no means do they express its essence. And so, the world known in these forms, i.e., the world that extends in space, changes in time, and is defined by categories of reason, is not a world of independent reality, but only a world of phenomena, i.e, of our representation. And aside from these phenomena we do not know and cannot know anything. All supposed knowledge of what objects are in themselves, i.e., independently of the necessary subjective forms of our representation, all such transcendent knowledge is *illusory* (*Schein*).

Everything that is existent for us, i.e., everything that is known by us, exists for us, i.e., is known only in certain forms and according to certain categories, which thus have the character of universality and necessity. Without these categories no knowledge, no experience, is possible for us. Clearly, these forms and categories cannot be obtained by us from experience, from external reality, for, since they are a necessary condition of all experience, they precede all experience. They are therefore the subjective forms of our knowledge, and, since that which exists is known by us only insofar as it is determined by these subjective forms, it follows that all that is known by us, *as known*, all the properties and relations known to us of that which exists, our whole world, is posited by our knowing subject, and outside of this subject there is no knowledge at all. Outside of it the existing independent reality—*Ding an sich*—is completely inaccessible to knowledge, is for us a pure X.

It must be noted that Kant's main proposition on the subjective character of knowledge and the complete inaccessibility for us of things in themselves, remains unassailable even if one rejects (as the most recent positivists do) the necessity and universality of our knowledge asserted by Kant, and recognizes our knowledge as being exclusively empirical, as being acquired from outside without any active participation of the knowing subject. For, even in this case, since it is assumed that what is known in itself abides outside of us and only acts upon us in an external manner, it is obvious that we can know not being in itself but only its action upon us or its manifestation in our consciousness. Therefore, together with Kant, the positivists assert that phenomena alone are accessible to us, whereas the essence of these phenomena is absolutely unknowable. The same thing must be recognized from the materialistic point of view. For if, according to the assertion of materialism, all thinking, and therefore all cognition, is only a physiological process in our organism, or at least is wholly determined by such a process, it is clear that our knowledge does not have any objective significance. For what can the infinite world of existing things outside of us (assuming such a world exists) have in common with some neural process in our body, some oscillations of brain matter molecules? A materialist too must necessarily accept Kant's proposition that objective being, as it is in itself, is absolutely inaccessible for us.

However, the system of transcendental idealism, in the form in which Kant left it, appears to be unfinished, to leave something unsaid. There are two unclarified points in it which should serve as the beginning of a new development. In the first place, in no wise could the concept of thing[38] in itself—*Ding an sich*—be retained. In Kant, this thing in itself, about which we can know nothing at all, is nevertheless considered to really exist outside of us, to act upon us, and with this action to produce in us that empirical material of sensation which, clothed in *a priori* forms of apprehension (space and time) and then in the categories of reason, forms the objective world of phenomena known by us, the domain of our experience. But affirming in this manner the thing in itself as existing and acting upon us, Kant attributes to it the qualitative category of existence (reality) and the relative category of causal action. However, according to Kant, all categories, and therefore the two noted, are only subjective forms of our knowledge, having a legitimate application only to the world of phenomena, the world of our experience. By no means can they be applied to the thing in itself, since it is something outside of experience. Therefore, by no means can one attribute to the thing in itself action upon us or even existence in general. That is, one must consider it as not existing. Therefore, Kant's successor in the philosophical development, Fichte, was fully justified in completely rejecting the assumption of a *Ding an sich* and, according to the principles of Kant himself, not acknowledging any independent existence outside of the knowing subject.

Another point of Kant's philosophy that is little developed in *The Critique of Pure Reason* is fully developed in Fichte and becomes the basic principle of his entire system, namely, the doctrine of the original synthetic unity of transcendental apperception.

All knowledge, all experience, is clearly possible only under the condition of the unity of consciousness in the knower, i.e., with the constant accompaniment of self-consciousness: I think. This act of self-consciousness, which conditions all experience, must be recognized as prior to all experience, i.e., as transcendental, and as such—in contradistinction to empirical consciousness, which is changeable and random—it gets in Kant the aforementioned name. Further, since, according to Kant, knowledge is the reduction of a diversity of sensuous data to the unity posited by transcendental apperception, the general forms of knowledge—the categories—are only the conditions under which the diverse material of sensuousness must be brought to the unity of self-consciousness. That is, the categories are only means of relating this unity to the multiplicity of empirical data. Therefore, Kant should have derived all the categories from the transcendental unity of self-consciousness, from the proposition *I am I* (I = I), as the primordial and fundamental condition of all knowledge. Defining the categories by functions of judgment and therefore deriving his twelve categories from twelve general forms of judgment, Kant should have shown how and why precisely such and so many forms of judgment follow from the transcendental act of self-consciousness. He should have shown how and why this transcendental act relates to its unity the multiplicity of empirical data in no other way than by precisely these twelve means. But Kant, asserting that the one basis of all knowledge, of all experience, is the synthetic unity of apperception, does not go beyond mere assertion and does not derive the actual forms of knowledge (the categories) from this synthetic unity of apperception, but instead takes them as given. Fichte, in his *Wissenschaftslehre*, develops Kant's principle into a complete and closed system. Having recognized the transcendental act of self-consciousness expressed in the proposition *I am I* as the one absolute principle of all knowledge, he *a priori* dialectically derived from it all the particular principles of knowledge. He thereby created the system of pure subjective idealism, for the proposition *I am I* is for Fichte not only a formal principle of knowledge. Because he rejected the reality of *Ding an sich* (the object outside of our consciousness), all that exists coincides for Fichte with the consciousness of the subject. He thus considers the transcendental unity of self-consciousness to be the absolute principle of all being, the primary creative act (*absolute Thathandlung*). The act of the self-positing of *I* necessarily contains the positing of *not-I* as well, which lays the foundation for the objective world. This world is only *not-I*. That is, it does not have any autonomous being, but exists only in relation to *I* and for *I*, as *I*'s necessary negation or limit, posited by *I* itself. Proper reality belongs only to the self-consciousness of the subject, for the pure *I*, the absolute act of self-positing, is found here. By contrast, objective nature, the world of the multiplicity of sensuous phenomena, as something completely posited by another, completely conditioned by consciousness (a consciousness that is already determined and conditioned), is, according to Fichte's expression, only the shadow of a shadow.

But it is obvious that Fichte's pure *I* cannot be identical with individual human self-consciousness, for the latter finds the objective world as already given, not as created by it, and itself as determined. And if, nevertheless, the world of the object as such cannot have autonomous being but must, according to its very concept, be posited by another, i.e., by the subject, this subject is not human, and its absolute act precedes our consciousness, in which it finds only its final expression. This is the meaning given to Fichte's principle by his successor in philosophy— Schelling. This completely changes the view of *nature*. When the significance of the absolute was attributed to the pure *I*, i.e., to the subject as only such, objective nature necessarily became only *not-I*, a mere negation or limitation (*Schranke*), without any autonomous being. It is otherwise for the *absolute* subject: In accordance with its absoluteness, the absolute subject refers equally to the human spirit and to nature. Only for us, for the conscious determinate subject, precisely because of its *particular determinateness*, does nature appear as the *other*, as external and negative, as dead matter. In itself, however, in its inner being, nature is just as alive and just as subjective (if one can use this expression) as the human *I*, for, like the spirit, it is a manifestation of the absolute subject, the difference being only one of *degree*. Therefore, in the absolute, *I* and *not-I*, the ideal and the real, spirit and nature, are identical. And this absolute subject, not being a subject in the narrow sense, i.e., as the opposite of the object, is thus the absolute indistinction of the two, and can be called the *subject–object*. Since it is, in essence, an *infinite* subject, it cannot have an object as *external* to itself, as a negation, or *Schranke*, in Fichte's sense. It *has in itself* the possibility of its objectivity. Positing itself *as something* (*als Etwas*), it becomes an object for itself, contemplates itself objectively. Thus, the absolute divides into that which is contemplated or the object (the real pole) and the contemplator or the subject (the ideal pole). It can be seen that here, at the first stage of the actualization of the absolute, the subject is totally determined by the object, and therefore it is subjective or ideal only relatively. The relation of the subject to the object here is therefore far from being true knowledge, but can be considered as only an unconscious, sensuous intuition (*Anschauung*). But the absolute is the infinite subject by its very nature, and, going beyond the first, imperfect stage of its actualization, it manifests its subjectivity or ideality in gradual objectivization–subjectivization, which is nothing else but the creative process of nature. In this process, at each new and higher stage, the subject is manifested with a more proper, i.e., ideal, character, and, at the same time, it includes all the preceding moments of development as its matter. Therefore, every moment of the process, every manifestation of the absolute, which signifies the subjective pole in relation to the preceding lower levels of development, itself becomes matter (the object) for the new, higher moment. This is the same relation as that between Aristotle's *dunamis* and *energeia*. The cosmic process reaches its culmination in human consciousness, in which nature is liberated from its reality, from its blind, elemental (although essentially spiritual, i.e., subjective) creativity. In human beings, the absolute subject–object appears *as such*, i.e., as pure spiritual activity, containing all of its own objectivity, the whole process of its natural manifestation, but containing it totally ideally—in consciousness. This ideal character belongs to consciousness *in general*, as such. But, in our usual or immediate consciousness, the relation to the object, being ideal in itself, is not *posited* as such. The object is taken as *external*, as a thing. However, in *philosophical* knowledge, ideality or freedom of consciousness appears *as such*. Here it is recognized that the subject that *knows* the natural process of cosmic evolution is the same subject that had been *accomplishing* this process. This subject knows here only its own activity as an objective activity (*sub specie objecti*). Thus, the original identity of subject and object is restored in philosophical knowledge. However, it is restored not as an empty nondifference but as posited and acknowledged, as having passed through difference and as having preserved itself in this differentiation and having returned from this differentiation to itself.

The progress of idealism compared with the system of the *Wissenschaftslehre* is obvious here. In Fichte, the subject was one-sided; it remained in itself and objective nature was only its negation. In Schelling, by contrast, the subject absorbs nature, so to speak, and nature then acquires a positive actuality, but only as a manifestation, a self-determination of the absolute subject. Referring to itself, positing itself for itself, the absolute subject then becomes an object or a reality. The process of natural development from gravitating matter to the most complex forms of organic life is the self-evolution of that spirit which in the highest moment of self-consciousness can say to itself:

> I am the God of the world, who cherishes it in his breast,
> The spirit agitated in nature.[39]

But if all that exists is, according to Schelling, the manifestation of the self-developing absolute subject (or subject-object), it is nevertheless necessary to differentiate (as Schelling indeed does; see, for example, his *Sammtliche Werke*, 1st ed., vol. 10, pp. 150–51) this very development, i.e., its forms or moments, from that which is developing, i.e., from the subject (*hupokeimenon*) of this development. This subject, leaving its nondifferentiation, is objectified gradually, moves and develops, passing from one form into another. As such, these forms are fully expressed logically in determinate concepts; they are thought. The subject (*hupokeimenon*) of all these forms cannot, in its essence, be expressed in any determinate, separate concept. What is this absolute subject principle of Schelling? The terms "absolute subject" and "subject–object" do not refer properly to this principle itself but are only definitions *per anticipationem*. For the subject–object or absolute subject, the *hupokeimenon*, appears only at the *end* of the cosmic process, as its final result, which already presupposes perfect objectivization-subjectivization. It goes without saying that, in itself, the subject (*hupokeimenon*) cannot be an actual *object*. But if it is not an actual object, it also cannot be an *actual* (*actu*) subject, for the one is correlated with the other and cannot exist separately. Thus, in itself, the absolute principle is neither an actual subject nor an actual object, and therefore it cannot be the actual unity of the two.

However, it is obvious that all that exists *actually* (in the usual sense of the word), i.e., immediately, must necessarily be a subject or an object, and, in correlation, both the one and the other at the same time. Therefore, the absolute principle in general is not something that exists *actually*. Consequently, it exists only in *possibility*, in concept. Not being anything actual, i.e., immediately existent, the absolute principle is pure possibility or pure concept. That is, it is not some determinate concept (for nothing determinate and, as such, *particular* can be an absolute and universal principle); rather, it is concept in general, concept as such, i.e., the very *form of concept*. And if all that exists is the self-development of the absolute principle, it follows that all that exists is the concept's self-development. All has its being only in concept, or all is the concept's being. Such is Hegel's principle. Truly, there is no actual existence in the sense of something subsisting or abiding independently of concept; it is only the product of a limited reason. There cannot be anything that exists immediately and substantially, for all is the becoming (*genesis*) of concept. Concept, as the German word (*Begriff*) shows, is, by its nature, not something subsistent or abiding, something immediately ready. Rather, it is nothing but the very act of understanding, the pure activity of thinking. But activity is impossible without differentiation, without splitting. Undifferentiated simple unity remains in itself, does not change, does not act, does not live: such is the uni-existent of the Eleatics and the substance of Spinoza. Concept, as pure activity, is eternally differentiated in itself, relates to itself negatively, posits itself as another, changes, passes into another in a multiplicity of moments. From this there comes that changeability, that constant transition of one thing into another, that flow which constitutes the being of all that exists, the life of all that lives. For all that exists is a manifestation of concept, while concept is, in essence, activity, activity is differentiation, and differentiation is negation, the positing of another. At the same time, however, this differentiation and negation are differentiation and negation of the concept itself. The concept itself posits itself as another, and this self-negation constitutes its whole essence as pure activity. Therefore, in changing, in positing another, the concept only expresses its own essence. It asserts itself as such through negation; that is, it becomes for itself a manifested concept, existing for itself. Thus, every change, every transition to another, is only a new triumph of the concept, which in each negation finds itself and returns to itself as a posited, expressed concept. And all that exists is this dialectical development of the concept, which in its immediate positing (the thesis: abstract unity, the rational moment) contains contradiction and therefore passes over to the opposite (the antithesis: reflection, the negatively rational moment). In this opposition, the concept finds its own essence and therefore returns to itself through negation of negation, but now as a manifested contradiction and therefore free from contradiction (the synthesis: the higher concrete unity, the positively rational, or speculative, moment). Content thus coincides with form. "The absolute idea has as content itself as infinite form, for it eternally posits itself as another, and again removes the distinction in the identity of the positer and the posited."

This system of absolute rationalism,[40] following necessarily, as has been shown, from the preceding philosophical development, concludes this development and does not allow further movement on this path. For the essence of Hegel's principle consists precisely in the fact that it expressly contains its negation within itself. Therefore, in this system, which has rejected the law of contradiction, it is impossible to indicate any internal contradiction that would stimulate the further development of the system, since any contradiction in the sphere of this system is posited by it as a logical necessity and is again removed in the higher unity of the concrete concept. This is therefore an absolutely perfect and self-enclosed system, and, by knowing it, we shall come to a better understanding of the general meaning of the whole intellectual development which found its culmination and self-definition in this system. For the character of philosophical rationalism (i.e., the assertion of concept as absolute *prius*), which was fully unfolded in Hegel, was already present at the very beginning of Western philosophy and, gradually evolving, finally led to Hegel's absolute *panlogism*. One can already see the first seeds of this tendency in medieval scholasticism. Further, in Descartes, it found expression in the assertion that all that exists is knowable in clear and distinct concepts (i.e., discursively), both in its objective content or *essence* (*essentia*) and in its *existence* (*existentia*). For, as Descartes says, if I clearly and distinctly think something as existing in a certain manner, it exists actually (outside of me), and it exists such as I think it.[41] But in asserting such an absolute knowability, Descartes posits that what is known nonetheless has independent existence outside of the knower. What is known is not only completely independent of the knower according to its *existentia*, but it is even, in part, completely heterogeneous with respect to the knower according to its *essentia*, for certain of the objects that are known, namely bodily or *extended substances*, differ *toto genere* from the knower as such, i.e., from the *thinking* substance. Cartesianism thus presents a two-fold dualism: first, between the knower and the known, which are, in general, mutually independent in their *existence*; and, secondly, between the knower as a thinking substance and the known as an extended substance, which in its *essence* has nothing in common with thinking. Thus, two questions arise: How can I know that which, in its *essence*, is completely different from me, the knower? That is, how can I know an extended substance? The second question is: How can I, in general, know that which is outside of me and *exists* independently of me, be this another thinking substance or a bodily one? The first question, the one concerning heterogeneous essences or natures, was resolved in the abstract identity of Spinoza's substance and in the concrete unity of Leibniz's monad. For Spinoza, thinking entity and extended body are identical; however, they have this identity not in themselves but only in the nondifferentiation of the universal substance, and therefore outside of their own actuality. This is a completely abstract identity. In Leibniz, the contradiction is resolved by rejecting the independence of extended matter with respect to the thinking substance and positing that this matter is only an object or representation of this substance. An extended material body is recognized as being a phenomenon (*phaenomenon bene fundatum*) posited by the active force of a monad. Thus, Leibniz completely resolves the first question by eliminating all *essential* (*essentialis*) heterogeneity, for, according to him, all entities are equally monads or representing forces, differing from one another only in *degree*. But even if difference in essence is removed, separation in existence remains, for, in Leibniz, what knows, even as such, is only an entity among other entities. Therefore, in its essence, what is known coincides with what knows, but, in its existence, it is completely independent of what knows. Thus, Leibniz's final resolution of the first question puts on the agenda the second question, which was then resolved by Kant.

Kant considered all that is knowable as such to be only a phenomenon, i.e., to exist only insofar as it is known, to exist only in the representation of the subject. That which exists independently of the subject, the *Ding an sich*, is absolutely unknowable, or it is known only insofar as it is determined by the subject. That is, the subject always knows only its own determinations, the forms of its own knowledge. Thus, to the question, "How can I know that which exists outside of me and independently of me?"— Kant gives the answer that I do not in fact know any of this, that all that I know exists only in me myself as my representation, produced by my cognitive functions, such that what is known is always only a product of my knowledge. All that is known is identified here with knowledge itself. But, outside of knowledge, as absolutely unknowable, there remains, on the one hand, the inner essence of external phenomena and, on the other hand, the inner essence of the subject itself, to which the knowledge belongs.[42] Kant accomplished a feat of gigantic abstraction: Knowledge as a form is completely separated from all content, which is posited outside of this form. Thus, on the one hand, we have the pure form of knowledge without any real content,[43] and on the other hand we have independent content, the *Ding an sich*, devoid of all form, absolutely unknowable. And this abstractness is seen as their necessary character, so that what exists is never expressed in knowledge and knowledge never knows what exists. But it is clearly arbitrary and meaningless to attribute existence or reality to this essence, which is absolutely unknown to us and about which we therefore cannot speak. For when I say, "X exists," if the subject of this sentence is absolutely unknown to me, i.e, if it does not exist for me at all, what, then, does the predicate express? Therefore, the further development of philosophy consistently rejected this unknowable. As we have seen, the unknowable object was rejected in Fichte, while the unknowable subject as something abiding by itself, a subject that was still present in Schelling, was definitively removed by Hegel. What remained was knowledge as absolute form, a pure act of conceptualization or thinking. Already in Kant, knowledge had become a pure form without any content; however, having outside of itself the existent reality as the absolutely unknowable, knowledge in Kant is completely deprived of true value. In Hegel, however, with the removal of all reality existing outside of knowledge, knowledge *as such* becomes the sole existent; it receives, nonrelatively, the significance of the absolute truth. Not having anything besides itself, it must be pure form and nothing more. It must be self-thinking—*tēs noēseōs noēsis*. This is not its limitation, as in Kant, but its absolute infinitude. The usual consciousness differentiates among the known object, as independently existing; the knower, also independently existing; and knowledge, as their relation. But, clearly, the *known object* exists only in the consciousness, for if it is posited as external, this externality is a determination of that very same consciousness, to the extent there is consciousness of it. By no means can I say that something exists *completely* outside of my consciousness, i.e., with no relation to it. For either I know that it is outside of my consciousness (but then it is already not outside of consciousness, for its externality is posited in knowledge) or I do not know about it. What am I talking about, then? Prior to Kant this same conclusion was arrived at by the Irish philosopher Berkeley. However, recognizing objects or things only as representations (or *ideas* according to the Anglo-French terminology), Berkeley kept the subject as *substance*. But the same argument can be applied to the subject: The subject too (i.e., I myself) exists only in self-consciousness, only insofar as I know about myself. The *I* itself is nothing other than the act of self-positing or self-consciousness. This is where Fichte stopped. But if the *I* exists only in knowledge, only insofar as it is known, it is clear that the *I* as an independent subject is the same sort of representation in knowledge as external things. Therefore, in itself, there exists only this knowledge, the very activity of thinking, positing in itself what thinks and what is thought. This definitively solves the problem of knowledge, for all duality between the knower and the known is removed. It is removed by the fact that both are annihilated as such, and there remains only the act of understanding, in which all contradictions are necessarily overcome. Concept, which in Descartes was posited as the absolute *prius* of *knowledge*, i.e., *for us*, becomes, in Hegel, the absolute *prius in general*, in itself, as the pure act of self-thinking, ideally containing in itself and really positing all that exists.

Hegel's philosophy, as a system absolute in its sphere, completely self-enclosed, cannot be rejected *partially*, i.e., developed. One can exit it only by recognizing the one-sidedness or limitation of its whole sphere or of its very principle, i.e., the principle of abstract concept, the sphere of pure logic. In fact, as soon as Hegel's doctrine was fully expressed and understood, it was immediately rejected in its absoluteness by a simple axiomatic assertion: *concept is not everything*. In other words, concept *as such* is not yet reality. (As *only* concept, it has reality only insofar as I think it, i.e., only in my head. A distinction is therefore made between subjective and independent reality.) Hence, *besides concept as form something other is required as reality*.

This requirement for autonomous, concept-independent reality concludes the age of purely logical or *a priori* philosophy. It lays the foundation for a positive philosophy and opens the door to empiricism. And it is natural that the first kind of empiricism to become dominant was the closest and most accessible one, the empiricism of the external, sensuous world—the domain of the so-called natural sciences. When the object of these sciences—material being—is posited as an absolute principle, i.e., when it is considered as the one, independent reality, we get the system of *materialism*. In fact, immediately after Hegelianism we see the domination of materialism, based on the empirical data of natural science and attributing to these data a meaning inappropriate to them—a transcendental, metaphysical meaning.

The basic principle of materialism, i.e., the attribution of the significance of an independent reality to material being, had already been rejected by Leibniz. It was cut at the root by Kant and finally destroyed completely by the great Fichte. At first glance it might seem strange (and contradictory to the rational sequence recognized by us in the development in philosophy) that, after all this, materialism reappears and becomes the dominant view. The representatives of materialism were and are, for the most part, not philosophers but empirical scientists, chemists and zoologists, for whom such things as the critique of pure reason or the *Wissenschaftslehre* can have no intelligibility. But this circumstance only explains the fact of the dominance of materialism; it does not legitimize this fact. But we know that, by its nature, all development inevitably experiences reactions, temporary turnings-back, although no previous stage of development is ever entirely restored in exactly its previous form. The latest natural-scientific materialism is far from being the same as the materialism of Gassendi or Hobbes, La Mettrie or Holbach. It has another basis and its own distinctive character. We have also seen that the absolutely antiempirical system of Hegel led to the necessity of empiricism in philosophy. And it is known that, when some principle must be manifested in an intellectual development, its full expression and complete development require that the bearers of this principle recognize its absoluteness and thus absolutely reject all other principles. Therefore, the representatives of the empirical principle in philosophy (and the first of these were the materialists) had to reject absolutely—in the name of their principle as an absolute one—the opposite principle: the *a priori* knowledge of logical philosophy. They had to reject this philosophy not only in its pretension to absoluteness, but also in that formal significance which indisputably and genuinely belongs to it. For from the fact that logical philosophy does not yield any positive content, it by no means follows that it has no significance. If nothing else, it always has the significance of being the negative criterion of the truth. Pure mathematics has even less positive content; however, no one in his right mind would dispute the absolute obligatoriness of its propositions. But just as it could never be the case that the sum of the angles of a triangle equals not two right angles but twenty right angles, that some geometrical figure could be bounded by a single straight line, or that twice five equals seventeen, so nothing could be true that contradicts the propositions of logical philosophy, for the foundation in both cases is the same: *a priori* and therefore absolute or apodictic necessity, by means of both analysis and *a priori* synthesis. Therefore, if it is asserted *a priori* by logical philosophy that external or material being, by its very concept, can by no means have independent reality, but is necessarily posited by another, then no empiricism can make the contrary true. But from their point of view the materialists could not admit this and, in the name of the supremacy of their principle, had to expressly reject the most obvious propositions of logical philosophy. But although such a war with logic was waged by staunch and fearless warriors (for example, Karl Vogt, who had unabashedly announced in print that he could never understand a single philosophical book, and that therefore all philosophy is nonsense), it could not last very long. For since, in itself, empiricism cannot provide any universal system, and since the task of materialism consists precisely in building a universal system on the basis of external empiricism, the materialists were forced to philosophize. Here logical necessity took revenge, and materialism quickly had to arrive at self-negation. How this happened, we shall see later.

We said that, when the acknowledged one-sidedness of Hegel's system and of philosophical rationalism in its entirety called empiricism onto the stage, naturally enough it was the simplest and most immediate empiricism that appeared—namely, external empiricism, which, when raised to the level of a universal system, gives materialism. But there is a more intimate and inner connection between Hegel's philosophy and materialism.[44]

As is well known, for Hegel all that exists and does not exist has three main phases or moments: the idea in itself, the pure logical concept; then, the idea in the external being of nature; and, finally, the idea which has returned to itself in the human spirit. Hegel took the first moment, i.e., the concept in itself, as the absolute principle. But since a concept as a reality is recognized as unthinkable without one who conceives it, the true bearer of the absolute idea is an actual human being.[45] But one cannot recognize a human being or a finite spirit as the absolute principle, the universal subject, for in Hegel the very concept of the human being already presupposes the being of *external nature*, which conditions him. Therefore, it remains but to recognize this external being of nature as the first, absolute principle. Such a recognition at once transforms everything into its opposite: the principle, the content, and, primarily, the method of knowledge. When the concept of reason, a principle internal to the knower, was taken as the absolute first principle, the method of knowledge too was internal, *a priori*, dialectical; however, when the being of a nature completely external to the knower as knower and independent of the knower became the absolute principle, knowing itself necessarily became external. If that which really exists is a nature that, in itself, is external for me, the knower, and is not determined in any way by my reason, then it is obvious that true knowledge does not derive *a priori* from my reason but is given to me from outside, in experience. That which I know as a manifestation of nature itself, as a fact, will be true. Therefore, the source of knowledge becomes external experience and the method of knowledge becomes inductive empiricism. With this, philosophy enters into the domain of the empirical sciences which study external phenomena.

But since the object of the empirical sciences is nature in determinate forms, these sciences do not provide the universal foundation that is sought. This foundation cannot be provided by any empiricism, but it can be derived from empiricism. One need only take the general content of all the forms known in science, and the universal foundation of nature will be obtained. This general content of all external forms is matter. Science does indeed employ a concept of matter, but the matter that science knows is qualitatively determinate. That is, it is extended, impenetrable, divisible, gravitating, and so forth. Thus, since all matter is reduced here to determinate qualities or relations, it can, in this form, by no means be the foundation that is sought. Therefore, one asks: What is the foundation of matter itself? The answer that materialism gives to this question is the concept of the *atom*, of indivisible units, which compose the manifested matter. But what is an atom? Either an atom is actually indivisible and therefore unextended, a mathematical point, a zero of space (in this case, atoms will never come to compose actual matter, for however many zeros one adds together, nothing but a zero will result), or it has a certain extension and therefore is divisible. But even if one admits the absurdity of a divisible indivisible thing, even that is insufficient for the formation of *empirical* matter. One must also recognize an atom as having a certain density, a specific weight, which, in chemistry, atoms are hypothetically considered to have. But here an atom loses all independent character, is completely reduced to external relations, becomes a mere *phenomenon*. Therefore, if the foundation of the objective world is matter, this world is only the world of external *phenomena*. Materialism thereby passes over into *positivism*. Here an obvious parallel emerges: Just as the rationalist realism of Wolff's philosophy necessarily led to Kant's rational criticism, so the empirical realism of the materialists necessarily led to Auguste Comte's empirical criticism. For all realism, i.e., all acknowledgment of independent reality behind an external object (be it an object of reason or a sensuous empirical object), is, in its essence, meaningless and an absurdity (*katexochēn*).

Thus, as is fitting, positivism considers the autonomously existing material being of materialism to be only an external phenomenon. A phenomenon is opposed to what is independent, to what exists in itself. Therefore, a phenomenon is what exists in and for another; it is a representation in consciousness. In his system of logic, the positivist Mill defines an actual phenomenon as *a state of our consciousness*. Here consciousness should, strictly speaking, be understood to mean sense perception, for positivism, taking as its point of departure solely the external empirical domain, considers all other content of consciousness to be empty abstractions without any reality. According to Comte, only that knowledge has reality (i.e., expresses an actual phenomenon) which can be reduced to the data of the external senses. Thus, the knowing subject itself actually exists only as an object of sense perception; it is only a complex phenomenon, conditioned by other phenomena. For that reason, Comte never speaks of our intellectual or moral being but only of the intellectual and moral *functions of the brain*. Thus, the knowing and willing subject—every consciousness—is only a function of the brain. But what is the brain itself with its functions? One of the physical phenomena. But what is a phenomenon? The state of our sensuous consciousness, our representation; therefore, the brain is one of our representations. Thus, the brain is also the subject of every consciousness, and at the same time that very same brain is one of the phenomena in consciousness. That is, it is one of the products of its own function. But if the subject of consciousness itself is only a phenomenon in consciousness, there is clearly no subject at all.

Rather, as Comte says, there are only states of consciousness by themselves, only phenomena, which are found in various external interrelationships of sequence and similarity.

Moreover, phenomena in general, as being that is not independent but conditioned by another, necessarily presuppose this other, i.e., something absolute or independent. And although positivism completely denies the knowability of this absolute, it asserts its reality. Herbert Spencer states:

> Although the absolute cannot be known in any manner or to any degree, we find, however, that its positive existence turns out to be an inevitable given of consciousness; that as long as consciousness continues, we cannot for a minute separate ourselves from this given; that the belief in this given has a more certain guarantee than any other belief."[46]

Thus, philosophy has once again come to that unthinkable dualism which we saw in Kant: on the one hand, the contingent being of phenomena, the only thing accessible to us, the world of our experience, our knowledge; and on the other hand, being in itself, completely inaccessible to us and absolutely unknowable. But from Kant to Comte the human mind did not labor in vain. When Kant proved that that which truly is, is unknowable as an object of reason, and when, after Kant, it was proved that that which is cannot, in general, be an object, there still remained the possibility of seeking that which is in the very process of purely logical, objectless thinking. But now, after the purely logical philosophy, fully developed by Hegel, has shown its limitations and been recognized in its one-sidedness to be only a formal philosophy, it is impossible to return to it in its former meaning. The positivists bluntly acknowledge that purely logical thinking is devoid of all real content, an empty abstraction.[47] It is also impossible now to seek that which truly is in the hypostasized matter of external experience, in atoms, for positivism originated in the self-negation of materialism, and although the positivists of the second rank usually take materialistic points of view, the true representatives of positivism—Comte, Mill, Spencer—consider matter or atoms to be metaphysical abstractions, devoid of all positive reality, like all the other substances or essences of the old metaphysics.

Philosophical thought in the phase or moment of positivism arrived at the following indisputable and highly important results: Independent reality or that which truly exists is neither the object of reason (for the object of reason is posited by reason itself) nor the concept in itself in the process of pure thinking (for this thinking cannot transcend itself, and therefore the pure concept is only an abstracted form, not yet having reality). Nor does the content of external experience constitute independent reality, for this content is only a phenomenon conditioned by our consciousness. Does it not thus simply remain to assert, with positivism, the absolute unknowability of that which truly is, of the basis of all phenomena? We have seen that such an absolute unknowability was asserted already by Kant, and we have also seen that this assertion does not withstand criticism. At the first contact with analysis, the absolutely unknowable essence—the *Ding an sich*—turns out to be a concept that cannot be conceived, i.e., just a meaningless combination of sounds. It is clear that it is impossible to consider the absolutely unknowable as that which truly is, i.e., to attribute a positive predicate to pure negation. In fact, strange to say, positivists do admit a certain knowability of the absolutely unknowable. Thus, Herbert Spencer, in the above-cited passage, where he says that the absolute cannot be known in any manner and to any degree, adds in brackets: "in the strict sense of the word *knowledge*." But if, therefore, the absolute is knowable in the *non*-strict sense of the word, and if this non-strict knowledge is nevertheless indisputably a certain manner and a certain degree of knowledge, then in no wise can one say that the absolute is knowable in no manner and to no degree. Absolute unknowability is thereby completely denied, and now the only thing that remains is to determine *what* this knowledge in the non-strict sense of the word is. Here it may turn out that the criterion that for positivism determines what knowledge is in the strict sense and what it is not derives from the exclusiveness and one-sidedness of positivism itself, so that for a more profound vision not only another relation, but the opposite relation might obtain.

The principle of positivism is external experience. True knowledge, knowledge in the strict sense of the word, is for positivism a knowledge that comes from external experience, and consequently a knowledge in which that which is known is an *external object* for the knower. Therefore, when, from the point of view of positivism it is said that the absolute is unknowable, this only means that it is not an object of external experience. And this is completely true, for, by its very concept, independent reality cannot be an external object, for every external object as such is only a representation, conditioned by the representing consciousness. Thus, the basic assertion of positivism reduces to the indisputable and important truth that *independent reality cannot be given in external experience.* Moreover, as we have seen, and as positivism justly insists, independent reality is also not given in *a priori* knowledge. It is given neither in abstract–rational knowledge (Wolff's dogmatism) nor in speculative–dialectical knowledge (Hegel's idealism). But if it is known neither in *a priori* thinking nor in external experience and at the same time cannot be unknowable, it is absolutely necessary to accept that it is known in *inner experience*, for there is as yet no other source of knowledge besides these three. Positivism asserts, however, that in inner experience, just as in external experience, we know only *phenomena*, not the entity in itself. This is completely true, and we only need to add what we have said a number of times, namely that such an entity, which abides exclusively in itself and is absolutely separate from all phenomena, outside of all phenomena, does not exist at all and cannot exist, just as there is no phenomenon and can be no phenomenon without the absolutely independent entity whose phenomenon it is. For even though it is possible and necessary to differentiate a phenomenon from the entity that is behind it, differentiation is not separation. Thus, for example, in any object one must differentiate form from content, but nobody in his right mind could imagine that the form of an object exists by itself, separately from the content, and that the content exists by itself, separately from the form. The independent entity behind the phenomenon is known only in the phenomenon. The assertion of Kant and Comte that we know only phenomena is more than an axiom. It is a tautology. For to be a phenomenon and to be known mean the same thing, namely, to be for another, in contrast to being in itself. And, clearly, this being in itself is conceivable only in opposition to phenomena, in self-differentiation from them, and therefore only in phenomena. Separately or *without* phenomena, being in itself is inconceivable. All that exists is known in phenomena, for all that exists *is* in phenomena. In other words, all that exists is in knowledge and, outside of or without knowledge, nothing exists, although knowledge is, of course, not yet all that exists, just as all that exists exists in a form, and nothing exists without a form, although the form is, of course, not yet all that exists. However, those who assert that we know only phenomena usually see in this a limitation of our knowledge.[48] But that is only because they think that phenomena do not express the independent entities behind them. In this way they separate the true nature of things from phenomena, the way a seed is separated from its shell. Against such a separation we must say with Goethe:

> Nature has neither kernel
> Nor shell:

> It is everything all at once.
> Examine yourself:
> Are you kernel or shell?[49]

Thus, the circumstance that in inner experience we know only phenomena by no means prevents us from knowing what is behind these phenomena, i.e., that which actually exists, *l'être en soi*. But in this case do we not directly know this *être en soi* also in the phenomena of external experience? By no means. This is the case not because they are phenomena, but because they are *secondary* phenomena. For in external experience we do not have a direct manifestation of that which actually exists for our consciousness; rather, we have a manifestation that is already diversely conditioned and determined. It is determined both by the empirical properties of our external senses and by the *a priori* forms of our reason, by the action or counteraction of which that which is, is manifested as an external or material object and therefore is not known in its inner essence. This externality, or materiality, is the veil that in external experience hides that which truly is from us. It is the curtain that separates reality from appearance, so that all that we immediately have in external experience is only our own representation. This deceitful veil is removed in *inner* experience. Being conscious of myself, of my own inner states, of my thinking and desiring, I clearly do not relate here to some external and therefore essentially unknowable object. Clearly, my thought or the action of my will does not exist outside of my consciousness of them, separate from them. All of their reality is therefore expressed in my consciousness of my inner states. I am conscious of them as they are, for outside of my consciousness they do not actually exist. Thus, in inner experience we already have not what is represented, or objects, but reality. It is clear that my thought, for example, in or for which all that is represented exists, cannot itself be represented. And, although in inner experience the knower is necessarily differentiated from what is known (for without such a differentiation no knowledge is possible), this differentiation is not an abiding, real, or objective one. It is not a separateness but a self-differentiation, which again is removed in the unity of self-consciousness. Thus, in inner experience we have the most immediate manifestation of that which actually exists. Here everything is reality.[50] Therefore, the positivists justly affirm that we cannot know the substance of our own spirit. Without doubt we cannot, for the sort of substance the positivists have in mind does not exist at all. Indeed, when it is said that we do not know our own essence, this essence is clearly assumed to be something that exists outside of consciousness, a substance completely separate from consciousness, some sort of unchangeably abiding reality or object in itself (*Ding an sich*). But an object in itself is a *contradictio in adjecto*, for objectivity signifies being for another, or representation. That which is in itself is also for itself. That is, it is manifested, differentiated in itself, or conscious of itself.

Therefore, even though knowledge is not essence but only the expression or form of essence, there can be no unknowable essence. Inner knowledge is true and real because there is no external object in it, because in it the knower and what is known do not abide outside of and separately from each other, but are merely differentiated. If by knowledge we mean (as the positivists necessarily do by the nature of their principle) only strictly objective knowledge, in which what is known is an external object or a separate substance, then, from this point of view, one must agree completely with Herbert Spencer when he says: "It is easy to prove that knowledge of self, properly so-called (i.e., objective), is absolutely denied by the laws of thinking."[51] "Thus," Spencer continues, "personality, of which everyone is conscious and the existence of which everyone considers a fact more certain than any other, actually cannot be known at all: knowledge of it is not admitted by the very nature of thinking."[52] To this one must add that not only the knowledge but also the *existence* of such personality is absolutely denied by the laws of thinking. For what in fact can be more absurd than a personality "of which everyone is conscious," i.e., which is known by everyone, but which, however, "cannot be known at all"? It is obvious that nothing like this exists or can exist in the nature of things. A real personality, our real essence, "of which everyone is conscious and the existence of which everyone considers a fact more certain than any other"—this, our true being, is by no means some sort of transcendent substance abiding outside of consciousness, the monstrous and stillborn child of an illegitimate union of crude fantasy and abstract reason. The true being of our personality is expressed and known in the reality of inner experience, in actual desire, in actual thinking, and in the actual permanent connection of the two in the unity of self-consciousness, which is precisely the actual *I*. Clearly, the immediate real content of our consciousness is not yet integral reality, is not that which is called absolute. The only thing that cannot be doubted is that, in our consciousness, we have a certain reality, a certain immediate manifestation of that which truly exists, and therefore know that which truly exists, even if this knowledge is not absolutely adequate at a given moment.

Thus, in our inner experience we find that which actually exists. But two basic elements or two aspects are distinguished in inner reality: the practical aspect and the theoretical one. We are conscious of ourselves as acting and as knowing. The general principle of all action is desire or will, while the general principle of all knowledge is representation. The question is asked: Which of these two elements comes first? Representation is a relation to another and therefore presupposes another, whereas will, even though it has a relation to another as to its object, is not itself a relation. Rather, as action out of itself and therefore self-assertion, it is independent by its nature, and therefore it is necessary to recognize *will* as the first principle. Thus, in our will we find the most immediate and accessible manifestation of that which is in itself, of independent reality. This is the principle of Schopenhauer's philosophy. We must consider this philosophy at greater length, both because of its originality (owing to which it cannot be subsumed under any general category) and because of the goal of the present inquiry, which is to explain the genesis of the contemporary crisis or revolution in philosophical thought. The origin of this revolution can be found in Schopenhauer, and Hartmann's system, which epitomizes the present instant of the philosophical consciousness, directly issues from Schopenhauer's doctrine.

The external objective world as it immediately appears in our sensuous consciousness is our representation. "If I take away the thinking subject," Schopenhauer asserts, using Kant's words, "the whole corporeal world will disappear, since it is nothing else but a phenomenon in the sensuousness of our subject, a certain kind of representation of the subject." This proposition is indisputably true, for it is self-evident that all that exists *for us* must be found in our consciousness, and it exists for us only insofar as we are conscious of it (an obvious tautology). The objective world immediately known to us is therefore only the world in our consciousness or our representation. Therefore, Schopenhauer could not have chosen a better proposition in the sense of absolute certitude than the one with which he begins the exposition of his philosophy: "The world is my representation." On the other hand, it is just as certain that the world in general is not only my representation, but also has an autonomous existence that is independent of my consciousness. But this essence is not given in immediate external experience. It must be *found*, and this finding is the task of metaphysics in general. The immediately objective world known to us is, as such, only our representation, and the philosophical investigation of this "world as representation" (*Welt als Vorstellung*) in its general character and forms must necessarily precede an investigation of its autonomous essence.

The world is a representation. A representation presupposes that which represents and that which is represented—a subject and an object. Division into subject and object is the first, necessary, fundamental, and most general form of representation. These two fundamental elements of representation are clearly correlative. That is, they exist only in relation to each other, presuppose one other, are inconceivable one without the other. An object is only the representation of a subject, while a subject is only that which represents an object. Further, since all represented objects are situated in space and time and we absolutely cannot represent any object without spatial and temporal determinations, it follows that space and time are necessary and general forms of the objective world. And since the objective world itself is nothing else but the representation of a subject, space and time are general subjective forms of representation, which thus necessarily condition all objective knowledge, all external experience. Space and time are presupposed by external experience and therefore cannot in any way originate in this experience. Space and time cannot be abstractions from external experience; rather, they are *a priori* necessary forms of our sensuous perception, according to Kant's definition.

If *time* were the sole form of our representation, no existence, nothing permanent or stable, would be possible. For the permanence of a phenomenon is known only from the contrast it offers to the change or succession of other phenomena that exist alongside or together with it. However, the togetherness of phenomena is not possible in time alone but is a determination of space. On the other hand, if *space* were the exclusive form of our representation, change, which is a succession of states, would be impossible; succession, however, is only an expression of time. Thus, these two forms of representation stand in contradiction to one another. That which is necessary in one is impossible in the other: Coexistence is impossible in time, while succession is impossible in space. However, our representations, the complex of which forms the real world, appear at once in both forms, and the organic union of the two is a necessary condition of reality. This union is produced by a special function of the intuitive reason,[53] which links the two opposite forms of sensuous perception in such a way that objective reality arises for us out of their interpenetration. This function of reason thus gives a new necessary and general form of representation, expressed in an abstract form as the law of *causality* ("the law of causality or the law of the sufficient basis of becoming";[54] Schopenhauer designates time and space as "the law of the sufficient basis of being"[55]—in what sense, we shall see below). This law determines the succession of states in time in relation to a certain space, so that the change which occurs according to the law of causality refers both to a determinate part of space and to a determinate moment of time. This gives what we call *matter*, which, as acting (and therefore changing) in space in a determinate manner, and also *abiding* in time, is therefore temporal in space and spatial in time, organically, inseparably uniting the two forms. Since matter appears only in action (we know matter only insofar as it acts), i.e, in the causal determination of one thing by another, it is nothing else but the objective expression of the law of causality. It is, as Schopenhauer says, "nothing but causality."[56]

Thus, the objective world contemplated by us is produced by means of the *a priori* forms of space, time, and causality. The material—and *only* the material—for this production consists of *sensations*. There is no possibility of producing—as sensualism wishes—the objective representation itself from only sensations and their combinations. All sensations are extremely poor in content, have a local, specific character, and are subject to only one general form—time. Moreover, they change within a very narrow range, and—the main thing—all of them are completely subjective, do not contain anything objective, and therefore cannot produce any objective intuition (*Anschauung*). Indeed, I have a sensation of light or of specific colors. I hear a sound, touch something hard or soft. All of these, for the time being, are only in me, are my subjective sensations, not giving any external object. Only when reason (through the application of the general *a priori* form of causality) represents these subjective sensations as *actions*, which necessarily have their *cause*, and when at the same time by means of space (a form just as *a priori*) this cause is represented outside of the subject as an external *object* that produces sensations (and reason uses all of the most minute data in sensations for a precise determination of spatial relations)—only then are indeterminate subjective sensations transformed into a determinate objective apprehension. It is clear that this whole process is accomplished not discursively or abstractly, but intuitively and immediately. Thus, this whole objective, material world, filling space in three dimensions and changing and moving in time according to the law of causality, this world with all the diversity of its content, with the unity and regularity of its form—is only a mental phenomenon. And, as such, this world exists only for us, in our perception. All that is objective is *eo ipso* something only subjective, for to be an object is to be only for the subject.

It is clear that the mental production of the objective world is not accomplished by the subject all at once. Only the formal part of the objective perception is found *a priori* in the mind, whereas the material, as we have said, lies in sensations, and the mutual determination of these two elements must be accomplished gradually. This explains the fact that determinate spatial and causal relations of the external world do not exist yet for the youngest infants. Such relations appear for them only when their reason begins to exercise itself on the data of sensation, predominantly visual and tactile sensation, and by means of this gradually produces a determinate objective world for itself. Thus, for example, when infants reach toward the moon, apparently wishing to grab it, it is clear that, although they see it outside of them, and therefore space in general exists for them (which indeed must be the case, since it is an *a priori* form), yet *distance*, i.e., a determinate spatial relation, is not yet found in their representation.

There are many facts that show empirically that external perception has a mental character. The fact that we see separate objects as *single* objects, whereas, because of the doubleness of the visual organ, there always exist only *double* visual impressions; the fact that we see objects in a position that is completely inverse to that in which we would see them if our sight were based exclusively on visual impressions,[57] and then the possibility of the stereoscope and, in general, the possibility of illusion or so-called sensory deception—all of these facts can be explained only by reference to the action of reason upon our sense perception. In general, after the psychophysiological investigations of Johann Müller, and, more recently, of Helmholtz, Fechner, and Wundt, the mental character of objective perception, proved by Schopenhauer *a priori*, must also be considered empirically proved, and constitutes an indisputable scientific truth.

Schopenhauer takes this intellectuality or subjectivity of the objective world as his point of departure in his critique of materialism. As a philosophical system, materialism is based on objective realism, i.e., on the view that attributes to the external objective world an autonomous reality independent of the representing subject, which, from this point of view, is only a phenomenon alongside other phenomena of the objective world. From this there naturally arises the tendency to derive the

subject from objective being as one of the forms or manifestations of the latter, which, indeed, constitutes the basic task of
materialism. Positing matter together with the forms of time
and space as existing by itself, and omitting the subject that
knows it, materialism at first tries to find the simplest state or
the first elements of matter. And then, by means of the law of
causality, taken as the absolute order of things in themselves, it
tries to gradually derive from these elements all the phenomena
and forms of nature, ascending from simple natural mechanism
to complex physical forces, then to chemistry, to vegetation, to
the animal world, and lastly to the final link of the chain—the
knowing human subject, who is thus only a modification of
matter, a special state of the latter. But, according to Schopenhauer, this is where the fundamental sin of the whole system is
revealed. Indeed, the final result, achieved with such labor—
our consciousness—was already presupposed at the very
beginning, with simple matter taken as the point of departure.
What in fact is this matter with all its states apart from our representation, in which alone and for which it exists? Our knowing subject is not only the final link. It also holds the whole
chain together. It is the bearer of the whole development, and
materialism is thus an absurd attempt to deduce that which
does the representing from its own representation.[58]

The external sensuous world is a concrete representation
produced by intuitive reason. To this world of concrete representations there is added, in human beings, the world of
abstract representations, general concepts, produced by reason
(*Vernunft*). According to Schopenhauer, reason is only the
capacity for abstraction, i.e., the separation of general features
from many concrete representations and their unification in one
general representation called a *concept*, which no longer has the
character of immediacy and cannot be perceived by the senses.
Although such concepts constitute the content of abstract

thinking, the mere existence of separate concepts in consciousness does not yet constitute thinking. Thinking requires that unification, that connection of concepts which is accomplished in *judgment* and conclusion. The formation of judgments is governed by a law which Schopenhauer calls "the law of the sufficient basis of knowledge."[59] This law states that, "in order for a judgment to express a certain knowledge, it must have a sufficient ground: only through this does it acquire the predicate of the true. Truth (in abstract thinking) is thus the relation of judgment to something different from it, which is called its ground."[60] Both concrete and abstract representations are thus determined only by different forms of the one law of sufficient ground, as a consequence of which the whole world of representation, both concretely perceived and abstractly thought, manifests itself as one whole with one general character. What is this character? What do we have in the world of representation? What is the value of this world?

Chapter II

As we have seen, the world of phenomena, in which we live and move, is determined by the general forms of space, time, and causality. We see that, on the one hand, these general forms of all phenomena constitute only modifications of the same so-called law of sufficient ground, i.e., the law of the determination of each phenomenon by another one. But, on the other hand, these forms are completely relative, for each of them expresses nothing more than a certain relation to another, a being for another. This is most clear in connection with the form of time. Here each moment comes into existence only by removing the preceding moment, and is itself then removed by the following moment, and so on, to infinity. The past and the future have no reality in the present, but the present itself exists only in relation to this nonexistent past and future, constituting nothing more than their common boundary, the mathematical point between them, in a word, a zero.

Similarly, the essence of space consists only in the possibility of the mutual determination of its parts, which is called *position*.

Every object has a position in space only in relation to other adjacent objects, which determine it. In itself, space is a pure void, nothing. Causality, again, consists in the determination of one phenomenon by another; it is the existence of one through another. Moreover, all three of these relations are general and necessary forms of the external or phenomenal world; only in them and through them does it receive its existence. From this it is clear why, in everything and everywhere, this world, without any doubt, is limited, impermanent, and dependent. In Plato's words, "origination and annihilation never appear in the capacity of essences."[61]

Hence, inasmuch as the world is determined by forms of representation, it (the world as representation) does not contain any genuine content, and nothing in it has real being. This necessarily leads to the question: *What* is real (*ontos*)? If the essence of the world does not consist in its objectivity, which, in itself, is completely empty, *in what* does this essence consist? This is the main question of metaphysics.

This question cannot be answered by abstract–logical means. Knowledge of metaphysical essence cannot be derived from general concepts, which, by their very nature, have no independent, primordial significance, since they are only abstractions from the data of immediate perception, external or internal. Similarly, metaphysics cannot be based on the *a priori* part of knowledge, since this *a priori* part has only formal significance. These are precisely those forms of perception and laws of reason which condition for the subject the possibility of all knowledge, create the world as representation, and cannot have any application outside of this representation. However, the task of metaphysics must be to transcend the world as representation. Therefore, metaphysics cannot be based on the formal subjective part of consciousness. Rather, it must be based on the content of consciousness. That is, it must have an empirical source of knowledge. In order to explain the real world contained in the totality of human experience, metaphysics must be based on this very experience, not on abstract concepts, which are devoid of proper content, and not on *a priori* forms, which have only conditional significance.

Thus, for the completion of the empirical task of metaphysics, we turn to the empirical domain and first to the external empirical domain. Its content—the external material world—is given to us immediately only as a phenomenon in the form of representation. How do we find here that which is not representation? As Kant proved, every given of experience consists of two elements: of general and necessary forms of our knowledge, conditioning the possibility of all experience and thus having an *a priori* character; and of the proper essence of phenomena (called *Ding an sich* by Kant), having an *a posteriori* character. To the extent that the given reality is determined by the first element, it is clear and understandable to us, for it is our own representation, a phenomenon in our consciousness. But to the extent that the second element is found in it, it is incomprehensible and mysterious for us. Identifying in a given phenomenon the general *a priori* forms of our knowledge, we get this second element, i.e., the inner essence of things, the unknown of metaphysics, but we get it as a pure unknown, as X, devoid of all *a priori* and therefore known coefficients.

If the world were determined exclusively by the forms of our knowledge, if it were only our representation, everything would be clear and understandable in it. All phenomena would be known *a priori*, by means of deduction from general forms of representation, and they would therefore be just as clear and simple as mathematical axioms and theorems. However, what we actually find is that, in every phenomenon, however simple it might appear, there is always something that cannot be deduced *a priori*, but is given to us empirically. There is always something that cannot be explained solely by forms of representation, and that therefore, from the point of view of representation, i.e., in immediate objective perception, is incomprehensible, mysterious to us. This incomprehensible and irrational element in any phenomenon is evidently its inner essence, the *Ding an sich*, which is independent of our representation and relates to the latter the way content relates to form. Therefore, the more incomprehensible some phenomenon is for objective apprehension, i.e., the less it is determined solely by general forms of representation, the more of the empirical element it contains, the greater will be the manifestation in it of the inner essence of the world, the *Ding an sich*, and vice versa. We find the same relation, of course, among the sciences that study the world of phenomena. The more *a priori* and therefore the clearer and more certain a science is, the less actual content there will be in it, the more formal it will be. The completely *a priori* and therefore the completely clear and certain science—mathematics—is also a completely formal science, exclusively concerned with representation in its forms of space and time, and not at all concerned with the inner content of these forms. In the phenomena studied by mechanics and physics, the formal aspect is still dominant, but here the empirical element is added. Although the laws of the motion that is studied in mechanics and physics, i.e., the general modes of the manifestation of motion, can be derived mathematically, i.e., *a priori*, nevertheless the essence of motion itself or of the forces of attraction and repulsion that condition it remains uncomprehended, both for immediate perception and for physical science, which explains only the *how*, not the *what* of phenomena. In phenomena of chemical affinity, the empirical element already gains an advantage over the formal element, and therefore chemistry has a much more irrational character than physics. In the organic world, science almost fully renounces *a priori* deduction. Finally, in human beings, the empirical element overshadows the general forms of representation to such an extent that, at first glance, the phenomena of human life proper appear not to be subordinate at all to these forms, not to have any basis conformable to law, so that, if, like all other objects, human beings were accessible to us only from outside, by means of reason with its general forms, they would seem to us a perfect miracle. But this miracle is we ourselves, and, thus, precisely here, where the forms of representation are a totally insufficient means of understanding, another source of inner and immediate knowledge is revealed to us—as a result of the fact that here the knower coincides with what is known. That purely empirical and therefore incomprehensible and mysterious element in all phenomena which constitutes their inner essence, this thing in itself, inaccessible to representation, the significance of which in the world of phenomena grows in proportion to their complexity and, finally, attains its *maximum* in us ourselves, as our own inner essence, and becomes accessible to us immediately—this element is transformed from X into a known quantity. All other objects are accessible to us only from outside, in forms of representation, whereas we are accessible to ourselves from within as well, from the subjective side in self-consciousness or inner feeling, where the independent essence is reflected in the most immediate way. In self-consciousness, this essence does not enter into the forms of external representation, but is known by us as our own will.

For our objective perception or external consciousness we ourselves are a representation alongside other representations, a material body in space and time, changing and acting like other bodies. The actions and changes of these other bodies are accessible to us only in external objective consciousness and therefore are unknown in their essence, for objective knowledge of an essence is inconceivable, since all that is objective is, as such, only a representation, a phenomenon by means of reason. But, besides being accessible to our objective perception, the actions of our own body are also accessible to us subjectively, in inner consciousness, since here we ourselves constitute what acts and not only what represents. I want to raise my arm, and I do. Here the same thing—the movement of my arm—that is manifested to external perception as the movement of a material object in space, in time, and according to the laws of mechanical causality, i.e., the same thing that is a representation, is, in inner consciousness, known immediately as an *act of will* that is not spatial and therefore is not subject to external perception:

> An act of will and an action of the body are not two objectively known states, united by a connection of causality; they are not in a relation of cause and effect. No, they are one and the same thing, only given in two completely different ways: on the one hand, in complete immediacy, and on the other hand, in apprehension for reason. The action of the body is nothing other than an objectified [*objectiviert*] act of will, i.e., one that has entered into perception.[62]

Thus, the inner essence, the being in itself of the motion of a body is an act of will. Or, more precisely, that which in a mediated manifestation, in an objective external perception or representation, is the motion of a body is, in its immediate manifestation, an act of will.[63] The knowledge that we have of our will is not, as we have said, a perception or concrete representation (for this is always spatial). Nor is it an abstract concept. On the contrary, it is more real than anything else. Furthermore, it is not formal *a priori* knowledge; rather, the data of inner experience are known here completely *a posteriori*. Therefore, it remains but to acknowledge that, in the inner consciousness of our will, we are immediately[64] conscious of the genuine nature of that which is—Kant's *Ding an sich*. If true essence, that which is not representation, is thus given to us only in inner consciousness, we must understand and explain the external world through ourselves, instead of under-standing and explaining ourselves through the external world.[65]

As we have seen, will is, first of all, expressed in voluntary movements of our body, insofar as precisely these movements are nothing else but the visible manifestation of particular acts of will. These movements simultaneously and immediately occur as one and the same thing as these acts of will. They differ from these acts only in the form of knowability into which they have passed when they became a representation:

> But these acts of will still have a foundation outside of themselves—in the motives of action. However, these motives always determine only what I will at a given moment, in a given place, under given circumstances, and nothing more. But that I *will* in general and *what in general* I will, i.e., the character of the whole of my volition, do not depend on them at all. Therefore, my will as a whole cannot, in its essence, be explained on the basis of motives, which determine only its manifestation at a given moment, are only occasions for expressing my will. Rather, my will itself is outside the domain of the law of motivation; only its manifestation at each moment is nec-essarily determined by this law.
>
> If now every action of my body is a manifestation of a certain act of will, in which, in the case of the given motives, my will in general and as a whole, i.e., my char-acter, is expressed, then the necessary condition and pre-supposition of bodily movement must also be a manifestation of will, for its manifestation cannot depend on anything that does not exist immediately and uniquely through it, on something accidental for it, through which its very manifestation would be accidental for it. And this necessary condition of all bodily movement is the body itself. Thus, the body itself must already be a manifestation of will and must have the same relation to my will in its entirety as separate actions of the body have to separate acts of will. The whole body must be nothing but the visi-ble appearance of my will, or my will itself, insofar as it is an object of perception, a real representation.[66]

For although it is indisputable that neither the organization of our body nor a significant part of its functions (the so-called involuntary or vegetative functions) depends in any way on our conscious will (i.e., that will of ours which is connected with the rational knowledge of motives), it does not follow that this organization is in no wise a manifestation or objectivity of will, and that these functions are not actions of will, since the concept of will, as we shall now see, cannot be confined within the bounds of empirical consciousness.

We have found in the inner consciousness of our will that which is not representation, that which expresses independent essence. However, it is clear that, in this unique given of immediate consciousness, in these narrow gates to the truth (according to Schopenhauer's expression), we have something completely ambiguous. For if, on the one hand, it is indisputable that our will, not being a representation, i.e., a being for another, is *eo ipso* an existent in itself, an independent reality, a *Ding an sich*, it is just as indisputable, on the other hand, that this will, as it is immediately known to us, namely, in the acts of will of separate empirical individuals, that this empirical will as such does not have any independent significance. For it is always determined by motives in the subject's consciousness, and the determination of the will by some motives or other depends on the particular character of each individual, while this character clearly does not depend on the empirical subject itself as such (the separate individual). That is to say, the individual will of empirical subjects as it is expressed in their separate actions is not independent or free; rather, it is conditioned. Since it is necessarily determined by motives in its manifestation, this will is subordinate to the law of sufficient ground as the fundamental form of phenomena, and therefore enters into the domain of phenomena. Will as we immediately know it, the will of human individuals, is always determined. Human beings, it is true, can act as they want, but this "as they want" is always conditioned; they want in this way or another, they want this or that, on the basis of these or those motives, which necessarily act upon them in conformity with their natural character, a character that does not depend on them.

On the other hand, the universal and indestructible consciousness of moral responsibility, which presupposes freedom, contradicts absolute determinism, for which this consciousness does not have any meaning. This consciousness is actually an indubitable and universal fact, which it is impossible to explain on the basis of any accidental or external causes. But, again, the necessary conditionedness, the lack of freedom, of the empirical will is just as indubitable a fact, recognized by both the ordinary consciousness and all true philosophers. This contradiction can be resolved only by differentiating will in manifestation from will in itself. This differentiation, expressed already by Kant in the doctrine of the empirical and intelligible character, was fully developed by Schopenhauer. In its essence, will is independent and thus free, but, in manifesting itself, it is necessarily subordinate to the law of phenomena, specifically to the law of sufficient ground. Therefore, every manifestation of will, every particular act of will, is necessarily always determined by the sufficient ground, can never be free, and determinism has dominion here. In its essence, will does not have any foundation outside of itself. It is autonomous or absolutely free; that is, it has a transcendent significance; it is a metaphysical essence. As such, it is all-one, for every real multiplicity presupposes space and time—forms that belong only to representation, not to that which exists in itself. If will is an all-one metaphysical essence, all that exists as a whole and every individual existence taken separately are only manifestations of this one will. That is, every particular phenomenon has a single independent will as its inner essence. Thus, all individuals who will are completely conditioned in their manifestations while being completely free in their inner essence. Although all of their actions are determined by motives, and the power of the motives over them is determined by their natural character, the latter is a product of their free will as a metaphysical essence. "All human beings are that which they are *through their own will*, and their character is primordial, since volition is the foundation of their being. They are their own work (*Werk*) prior to all knowledge."[67] Thus, by transferring the freedom of the will from the domain of the *operari* of the will (where those who acknowledged it placed it and where determinists justly denied it) to the domain of its *esse*, we resolve the antinomy of freedom and necessity and completely reconcile the opposing views.

Thus, will, when it manifests itself, is subordinate to the law of necessity, but, in itself, it is a metaphysical, all-one, absolutely free essence. There is a purely empirical element, not decomposable into forms of representation and therefore incomprehensible, which is intrinsic to every phenomenon of the external world and which, in the domain of external experience, physical science calls the forces of nature. ("Force" is taken here to mean an essentially unknown principle of phenomena, which, as we have seen, is the same thing as Kant's *Ding an sich*.) Because of the given inner experience, this element becomes completely known when it is determined as will. The category of force is thus reduced to the category of will and is thereby explained. This is not a mere change in terminology, but a real explanation of the unknown based on the known. For force is only the algebraic symbol for an unknown quantity, X, while will is what we know best, and, moreover, we know it not abstractly and formally, but immediately, as a genuine reality. Thus, on the one hand, all that exists is will, while, on the other hand, it is representation, determined by the general form of representation—"by the proposition of sufficient ground." Therefore, on the one hand (inwardly), all motion and change in the whole world of phenomena are the action of will as the first principle of all phenomena, while on the other hand (when they enter into the domain of representation), they are necessarily conditioned outwardly by a determinate particular *cause*. For the proposition of sufficient ground, with reference to motion and change, is the law of *causality*, or the proposition of the sufficient ground of *becoming* (*des Werdens*). The usual point of view recognizes two completely separate principles of motion: Certain motions, namely conscious human actions, it attributes exclusively to the inner principle of will and considers arbitrary. Other motions, namely motions of the material world, it just as exclusively attributes to external causes, which determine these motions with absolute necessity in contrast to the freedom of the first kind of motions. Schopenhauer, on the contrary, asserts that the two principles, together and inseparably, condition every motion, be it the falling of a rock or a human action, so that, strictly speaking, there are not two separate principles of motion, but only one, which is known in two different aspects. For every motion is jointly and equally conditioned, on the one hand, by will, as the *essence* of all phenomena without exception, and, on the other hand, by causal necessity, as the *form* of all phenomena without exception.

The error of the usual point of view is explained, in the first place, by the fact that the inner principle of all motion is known to us immediately only in ourselves, as our will, whereas, in the phenomena of nature, known only outwardly through representation, this inner principle, conventionally called a force, remains completely unknown. Therefore, one cannot acknowledge its essential identity with our will, an identity that is revealed only through philosophical reflection. Secondly, the principle of motion in its external aspect—causality—appears in different forms in different spheres of being, and with greater or lesser clarity. Thus, in the inorganic world, where it has the form of mechanical causality, it appears with maximal clarity because

cause and effect here are completely homogeneous and isometric, action is always equal to reaction, the quantity of motion transmitted is always equal to the quantity of motion lost. In the organic world, in phenomena of vegetative life, causality is no longer so clear, for here cause, appearing in the form of excitation (*Reiz*), differs both qualitatively and quantitatively from motion. Even less clear is the causal connection in phenomena of animal life proper, where cause takes the form of *motive*, and finally in human actions, which are also determined by motives, but where these motives are not only related to sense perception as in animals but are now also related to abstract thought. Here, although the law of causality does not lose its essential character, yet because of the complete heterogeneity of cause and effect, the connection between them becomes extremely unclear, even vanishing for the rough gaze, as a result of which the meaningless doctrine of the perfect freedom of human actions—*liberum arbitrium indifferentiae*—becomes possible.

Through the union of external and internal knowledge Schopenhauer's philosophy makes it possible to

> . . . recognize, despite all the adventitious differences, two identities, i.e., the identity of causality with itself at all stages, and then the identity of the initially unknown X (i.e., the forces of nature and life) with will in us. We know, I say, first the identical essence of causality in different forms, which it must assume at different stages, whether it appears as a mechanical, chemical, or physical cause, as excitation, or as an abstract, conceptualized motive (a motive of thought). We know it as one and the same thing, both where an impacting body loses the same quantity of motion as it transmits, and where thought struggles against thoughts, and the triumphant thought, as the strongest motive, sets us in motion, which motion is then effected with a necessity as great as that of the motion of a thrown ball. Where we ourselves constitute that which is moved and therefore the inner side of the process

is known to us with complete immediacy, we are not blinded and perplexed by this inner light. We are not alienated from the general causal connection presented to us in all of nature, and thereby forever deprived of the possibility of understanding it. On the contrary, we add a new, inwardly acquired, knowledge to the external knowledge, which serves as the key to the latter, and we know a second identity—the identity of our will with that X hitherto unknown to us, which had been a remainder in any causal explanation. As a result we say: There, too, where the most evident cause produces an effect, the mysterious thing that nonetheless remains there, that X, or the properly inner principle of the process, the true motive force, the existent-in-itself of this phenomenon (given to us, after all, only as a representation according to the forms and laws of representation) is essentially one and the same thing as that which, in the case of the actions of our body (also given to us as a perception or representation), is inwardly and immediately known to us as will. Therefore, just as we recognize the essence of causality (which has maximal clarity only at the lower levels of the objectivization of will, i.e., nature) at all stages, even the highest, so we recognize the essence of will at all levels, even the lowest ones, although only on the highest level do we immediately acquire this knowledge. The old error says: Where there is will, there is no causality; where there is causality, there is no will. But we say: Wherever there is causality there is will, and nowhere does will act without causality. Therefore, the *punctum controversiae* is: Can and must will and causality be present, at the same time and together, in the same process? An affirmative answer is made difficult by the circumstance that causality and will are known by two essentially different means: Causality is known completely externally, totally through mediation, totally through reason, whereas will is known completely inwardly, immediately. Therefore, the clearer in any given case the knowledge of the one is, the more obscure will the knowledge of the other be. Where causality is most comprehensible, there we least know the essence of will;

and where will is certain, causality is so obscured that crude reason decides to deny it. But causality, as we are taught by Kant, is nothing else but the *a priori* form of our reason, and therefore the essence of representation as such, which is one side of the world. The other side is will: it is *Ding an sich*. The clarification of causality and will, found in an inverse relationship, the alternating disclosure and concealment of the two, thus depends on the fact that the more something is given to us as only a phenomenon, i.e., as a representation, the more the *a priori* form of representation, i.e., causality, will be disclosed. On the contrary, the more immediately we are conscious of will, the more the form of representation, causality, will recede; that is how it is in us ourselves. Thus, the more one side of the world comes to the fore, the more we lose sight of the other side.[68]

All individual being, as such, is only a manifestation of one will, a manifestation conditioned by the forms of phenomena, i.e., space, time, and causality, which thus constitute that which the scholastics called *principium individuationis*. The multiplicity of individuals is only a phenomenon; in their separateness, they only appear, while the inner essence of all of them is identical. This essential identity of individuals and the illusoriness of their separateness find their natural expression in the life of the human race, while the moral consciousness of this identity is immediately expressed in the sympathy of an individual being for others. Schopenhauer posits this sympathy as the primordial foundation of all morality. To understand the significance of this principle, we must learn what character Schopenhauer considers to belong to will in itself.

Will, or volition, presupposes an object of volition. But the cosmic will, as the essence of all, cannot have any object outside of itself. Therefore, it can will only itself and is thus necessarily the will to one's own existence—*Wille zum Leben*. But, by its nature, all will is an unsatisfied yearning, a dissatisfaction.

Therefore, infinitely asserting its existence as will, the cosmic will infinitely asserts its dissatisfaction and is thus infinite suffering, eternal hunger. As long as will exists, in whatever forms it may be manifested, it necessarily remains unsatisfied yearning. Thus, all that exists, having will as its metaphysical foundation, is essentially suffering. If that is the case, the identification of one's being with another, i.e., sympathy, is necessarily co-suffering. Schopenhauer reduces all morality to sympathy or co-suffering.[69] It, in turn, has its metaphysical foundation in the essential identity of all that lives, for it is precisely in sympathy that this identity is affirmed by a moral being, which, penetrating (*durchschauend*) the *principium individuationis*, rejects this manifested, apparent individuality. This being stops considering other beings to be really separated from and external to it, and instead recognizes their existence as its own:

> And if this penetration of *principii individuationis*, this immediate knowledge of the identity of the will in all of its manifestations attains a high degree of clarity, it will at once exert an even more extensive influence on the will. That is to say, when the *principium individuationis*, this veil of Maya, becomes so transparent to our eyes that we no longer make the egoistic distinction between ourselves and others, but concern ourselves just as much with the sufferings of others as with our own, it follows naturally that we, knowing ourselves, our most inward and true *I*, in all beings, *must* also recognize as our own the infinite sufferings of all that lives and thus take upon ourselves the sorrow of the whole world. Now no sorrow is alien to us. Unlike one who is still subordinate to egoism, we no longer have in view only our own personal and changeable good and grief. Since we have been penetrated with the *principium individuationis*, all is equally close to us. We know the world as a whole, fathom its essence, and find it in constant disappearance, insignificant striving, inner antagonism, and constant suffering. Wherever we look we see suffering humanity and suffering animalkind, and the

perishing world. And all this is now as close to us as an egoist's own person is to the egoist. With such knowledge of the world, how could we now affirm this very same life by constant acts of will? Thus, if we who are still subordinate to the *principio individuationis* know only separate things and their relation to our person, and they then become constantly renewed *motives* of our will, then, on the contrary, the knowledge of the whole described above by us, of the essence of things in themselves, becomes a sedative for all and every will. Will now turns away from life. We attain the state of voluntary renunciation, resignation, true indifference, and complete will-lessness. Our will is converted; it no longer affirms its own being, reflected in phenomena, but renounces it.[70]

Here simple morality becomes asceticism, where the cosmic will is negated in itself as such, as the will to life, and everything that exists is rejected as its phenomenon. The goal is pure nothing, nirvana. To those who fear such an outcome Schopenhauer explains that *nothing* is a completely relative concept, which has meaning only in relation to the *something* negated by it. This *something*, i.e., that which we take to be positive and refer to as existent, is the world of representation contemplated by us and the will, constituting our own essence, which is manifested in this world. For this point of view, the negation of the will and its manifestations is nothing. But for another point of view the will itself with its manifestations can be nothing, and its negation can exist. Schopenhauer says in conclusion:

> Remaining entirely with the point of view of philosophy, we must be satisfied here with negative knowledge, having attained the final limit of the positive. Having come to know the inner essence of the world as will, and having recognized only the objectivity of this will in all phenomena, from the unconscious striving of the dark forces of nature to human activity full of consciousness, by no means will we avoid the consequence that, together with

the free negation, the self-annihilation of will, all those phenomena will disappear too, that constant striving and attraction without aim and repose at all the levels of objectivity, in and through which the world consists. The diversity of successive forms will disappear; together with will, its entire manifestation with its general forms (space and time) will disappear; and lastly, the final, fundamental form of this manifestation—subject and object—will disappear. If there is no will, there is no representation, no world. Before us there remains only nothing, of course. But that which resists this transition to nothingness—our nature—is, after all, only this very same will to existence (*Wille zum Leben*) which constitutes us ourselves and our world. The fact that we are so afraid of nothingness, or (which is the same thing) that we so desire to live, means only that we ourselves are nothing else but this will to life and know nothing aside from it. Therefore, that which will remain after the complete annihilation of will is, for us who are still full of will, nothing, of course. But, on the contrary, for those in whom will has undergone a conversion and renounced itself, this so real world of ours, with all its suns and milky ways, *is nothing*.[71]

That is the conclusion of Schopenhauer's philosophy. His affirmation of will as the fundamental principle, and the union of ethics and metaphysics which proceeds from it, signify, as we shall see, a complete reversal in the course of Western philosophy. But, for Schopenhauer, will as a metaphysical entity does not have any real meaning. For will in general, without any object of volition, without an aim, will without representation (which for Schopenhauer is not a necessary property of will but an accidental phenomenon or even, as he says, a *Gerhirnphänomen*), is clearly an empty word, not superior in any way to Kant's *Ding an sich* or the "forces of nature" in natural science. To give will its true significance and thereby to transform Schopenhauer's doctrine, removing its one-sidedness, constitutes Hartmann's task in his "philosophy of the unconscious," to which we now turn.

All volition wills the transition from the known present state to another state. A present state is given every time, even if it be merely repose; but volition could never be contained in this present state alone if at least the ideal possibility of something else did not exist. Even a volition that aspires to the continuation of the present state[72] is possible only through a representation of the cessation of this state, and therefore through a double negation. There is thus no doubt that for volition two conditions are necessary before everything else. The first of these conditions is the present state as the point of departure. The other condition, as the goal of volition, cannot be the present state, but is some future state, whose presence is desired. But since this future state cannot *really* be found in the present act of volition, but nonetheless must be found in it in some way (for without this state volition itself is impossible), it must necessarily be contained in it *ideally*, i.e., as *representation*. Likewise, the positively thought present state can become the point of departure of volition only insofar as it enters into representation. Therefore, *there is no will without representation*; as Aristotle was known to say: "There is no strong urge without imagination."[73] It is the failure to recognize this that gives rise to the peculiar character and one-sidedness of Schopenhauer's philosophy, which acknowledges will alone as the metaphysical principle, whereas representation or intellect is generated materialistically.[74]

Thus, the metaphysical principle is will united with representation. It is *representing will*. But will and representation are immediately given to us only in the consciousness of individual beings; and here, being completely conditioned, they clearly already belong to the world of phenomena. However, will and representation as the universal first principle lie beyond the limits of individual consciousness, and since we have no conception of the nonindividual consciousness, Hartmann defines his metaphysical principle as "the unconscious" (*das Unbewusste*). This term refers not only to the negative predicate "to be unconscious," but also to the unknown positive subject to which this predicate belongs, precisely instead of "the unconscious will and the unconscious representation," taken together.[75]

Although the metaphysical principle essentially lies beyond the limits of empirical consciousness, nevertheless, in the domain of this consciousness, in the domain of our experience, we can find data which, by their existence, presuppose and therefore require that we acknowledge this metaphysical principle. If there exist in nature phenomena which, being completely unexplainable by material or mechanical causes alone, are possible only as acts of a spiritual principle, i.e., will and representation; and if, in the case of these phenomena, it is certain that no individual conscious will and representation is acting,[76] then we must recognize these phenomena as the acts of a certain will and representation lying beyond the limits of individual consciousness. We must recognize them as the acts of that principle which Hartmann calls "unconscious" and which, not given immediately in the consciousness, is thus known in its manifestations, which necessarily presuppose it. In fact, Hartmann indicates such actions of the metaphysical spiritual principle in different spheres of experience, both external and internal. And, thus, on the basis of indisputable factual data, he proves the reality of this metaphysical principle by means of the inductive natural-scientific method.

Hartmann expresses the results of his empirical investigation in the following propositions:

1) The unconscious forms and preserves the organism, heals internal and external damage to the organism, purposefully directs the organism's movements, and conditions its employment for conscious will.

2) In instinct, the unconscious gives to each creature what it needs for its preservation that its conscious thought cannot provide. For example, to human beings it gives instincts to understand sense perception, to form language and society, and many other instincts.

3) The unconscious preserves genera by means of sexual attraction and motherly love, ennobles them through choice in sexual love, and steadily leads the human race in history toward the goal of its possible perfection.

4) The unconscious often guides human actions by means of feelings and premonitions in cases where conscious thought cannot help them.

5) By its suggestions in what is great as well as in what is small, the unconscious facilitates the conscious process of thought and, in mysticism, leads human beings to the presentiment of higher, suprasensuous unities.

6) The unconscious endows people with the sense of beauty and a feeling for art.[77]

In all of these actions, the unconscious is characterized by the following negative properties:

1) The unconscious does not suffer.[78]

2) The unconscious does not interrupt its own activity.[79]

3) Whereas all conscious representations have a sensuous form, unconscious thought can only be nonsensuous (*kann nur von unsinnlicher Art seyn*).

4) The unconscious does not vacillate and does not doubt. It does not need time to deliberate, but instantaneously grasps the result together with the whole logical process that produces it. That is, the thought of the unconscious is completely inner and immediate, like an intellectual intuition. Because of the coincidence of a thought process and its results at a single moment, i.e., in a zero of time, the thought of the unconscious is timeless (*zeitlos*), although it is found in time, insofar as the moment in which the thought is thought has its temporal place in the remaining series of temporal phenomena. But once we understand that this moment is known by us only through the manifestation of its result, and that the thought of the unconscious in each particular case acquires existence only by entering in a determinate manner into the world of phenomena (for it

does not require preliminary considerations and presuppositions), it is easy to conclude that this thought is found in time only insofar as its manifestation is found in time (*das In-Erscheinung-Treten*). But, aside from this, in itself, the thought of the unconscious is not only timeless; it is also nontemporal, i.e., outside of all time. In this case there can be no question of the representing *activity* of the unconscious in the strict sense, but it must be admitted that the world of all possible representations is confined, as an ideal existence, in the bosom of the unconscious. And *activity*, which by its very concept is something temporal, or at least something that posits time, begins only when, and as a result of the fact that, from this reposing ideal world of all possible representations, one representation or another enters into a real phenomenon, is posited by will as its object. Through this, the realm of the unconscious would be understandable as Kant's intelligible world.

5) The unconscious does not err.

6) Memory, comparisons, experiences cannot be attributed to the unconscious. It thinks everything *implicite* at a single moment. It cannot be perfected. It is always perfect.

7) Will and representation in the unconscious are connected in inseparable unity. Nothing can be willed that is not represented, and nothing can be represented that is not willed.[80]

Thus, the unconscious spirit undoubtedly has the significance of a first principle. On the other hand, consciousness as we know it, i.e., the actual consciousness of individual beings, obviously does not have the significance of a first principle, since it is conditioned by the existence of separate individuals and thus already presupposes the world of real phenomena. But this real world itself, matter itself, is only a manifestation of the same spiritual principle (unconscious will and representation), a principle which lies beyond empirical consciousness. Indeed, according to the usual conception, matter is a complex of atoms characterized by forces of attraction and repulsion. But a material atom, as was shown previously and as Hartmann explains in detail, is some-thing completely absurd. Matter is therefore reducible to atomic forces. What for another, from the outside, is force, in itself, from within, is will. And if it is will, then it is also representation. In fact, the atomic force of attraction or repulsion is not a mere ten-dency or striving, but a completely determinate kind of tendency (the forces of attraction and repulsion are subordinate to strictly determinate laws). That is, it contains a certain determinate direction, and this direction is contained in it *ideally* (otherwise it would not be the content of a *tendency*), i.e., as representation. Thus, atoms—the basis of the whole real world—are only ele-mentary acts of will, determined by representation, acts, of course, of that metaphysical will and representation which Hart-mann calls "unconscious." Since both matter and individual con-sciousness are therefore only forms of the manifestation of the unconscious, and since it is absolutely nonspatial, for it is what posits space (ideal space is posited by representation, real space by will), the unconscious is then the all-embracing single being, *which is all that exists*. The unconscious is the absolute indivisible, and all multiple phenomena of the real world are only acts and combinations of acts of this all-one being.[81]

The acts of the metaphysical entity—the world of phenom-ena—constitute a series of ascending development from inor-ganic matter to the higher organisms and humanity. Since what acts is a spiritual principle—the representing will—we can consider completely legitimate the question of the goal of this whole development, of the meaning of the cosmic process, of its beginning and outcome. Although Hartmann does pose this question, his answer to it, his cosmogony and eschatology, so clearly contradicts his own principles and represents such a striking *lapses angina* that his followers had to maintain the most profound silence about this part of his system. Not being members of their circle, we, however, must say a few words about these lamentable speculations.

The actual world has at its basis the representing will in the actual state, existing (*existens*) will. But actuality, act, presupposes possibility, potentiality. This logical order, according to which potentiality is conceived as preceding act, is boldly transformed by Hartmann into a factual order, and he very freely and easily asserts that the world will was *originally* (*ursprunglich*) found in a state of pure potentiality, a state of absolute nonvolition, i.e., a state of nonbeing (for the being of will is volition); and since the ideal principle (representation) acquires actual existence only from the real principle (will), the idea was also "originally" found in a state of pure possibility. That is, to say it simply, "originally" nothing at all existed, for being in possibility (*dunamei on*) is equal to nonbeing (*mē on*).[82] And since it is clear that pure nonbeing can by no means become *sua sponte* actual being (only the *concept* of nonbeing becomes the *concept* of being, and vice versa, as shown by Hegel, but the concept of nonbeing is not nothing, but precisely a concept), then, having posited pure nonbeing as the absolute principle, one should not have gone beyond this principle. But Hartmann, hypostasizing the concept of nonbeing or pure potentiality, speaks of it as of something existing and describes its arbitrary transition into a state of actuality. This begins the actual being of the world, which then, by a complex process of development, must again return to the original state of nonbeing. And Hartmann considers that this final transition to nonbeing—the goal of the cosmic process—must occur *historically*, as a future *event*.

We will not dwell on the particulars of this theory: their absurdity is too obvious. We consider it much more useful to *explain* their origin by indicating that property of thought which makes them possible, and which belongs not only to Hartmann, but to a greater or lesser degree follows from the one-sided character of all Western philosophy.

Chapter III

At the end of the previous section, I remarked that the basic cause of the alogisms that we encountered in Hartmann's philosophy has a general significance for all of Western philosophy. Indeed, this significance is included in the properties of *rational*[83] thought in general.

Abstract, or rational, knowledge consists in the decomposition of immediate, concrete apprehension into its sensuous and logical elements. These elements do not exist by themselves in separation; they exist only in combination, forming the actual world. This is perfectly clear in the lower, primitive spheres of being and knowledge—in the domain of external sense perception. Thus, for instance, it is perfectly clear that those quantitative and qualitative determinations which constitute a material object, such as shape, size, mass, color, and so forth, do not exist by themselves in separation. They exist only in a determinate combination, forming a concrete sensuous perception, what is called a real object. The separateness of these elementary properties is only a result of rational abstraction. The same is true for all other determinations, as well as for the most complex categories of logic or metaphysics. Each of these categories, taken separately or in itself, is only an abstraction. It becomes real only in combination with or in relation to other determinations, although this relative character is not always so clear as in the example presented. However, the essence of rational knowledge consists precisely in the analysis, or decomposition, of the concrete, i.e., in the fact that the categories or generating principles of what exists are *separated out*, are posited in themselves. If the exclusiveness of rational knowledge is not removed by a higher kind of thought, these categories, being taken in their separateness, naturally present themselves as existent in themselves as such. That is, they are hypostasized. Actual being is attributed to them, a being which they do not have in their separateness. This hypostasization of abstraction thus follows necessarily from rational knowledge in its exclusiveness, for, remaining itself, it cannot relate to itself negatively, cannot recognize the results of its activity as only abstractions or one-sidednesses. It necessarily attributes the fullness of actuality to them. The necessary moment of decomposition or abstract being for itself is obviously expressed here. But rational thought is a *stopping place*, the exclusive self-assertion[84] of this moment, which in that which actually exists, and therefore in true knowledge, is only a necessary transition. In the historical development of consciousness, the moment of rational thought and its necessary outcome—pure reflection[85]— is represented by Western philosophy. I do not mean by this that all Western philosophy has been limited to rational thought: history is not only a repetition of logical moments in all their purity. But there is no doubt that rational thought and abstract analysis predominate in Western philosophy. All the other tendencies of thought in Western philosophy appear only as reactions or protests against the dominant tendency, and therefore are distinguished by a similar one-sided limitedness, bear clear traces of the soil from which they have been separated.

At the very beginning of Western philosophy, in scholasticism,[86] rational thought appears in all its force. To the dominant school of medieval philosophy the world appeared as a dead collection of diverse substances (*entitates*), abiding outside one another, substantial forms, *universalia* of thought *ut realia*—all this without any inner connection. However great the significance in other respects of the revolution accomplished in Western philosophy by Descartes, the form of rational abstraction remained dominant in the new philosophy as well. Descartes himself recognized the presence of an independent reality behind the infinite diversity of separate substances or things, some of which are *only* extended substances while others are *only* thinking substances. Thus, the essential character of the scholastic world-view was fully preserved. Therefore, despite the blows that Spinoza, Leibniz, Bacon, and Locke struck against it, scholasticism was reborn in the eighteenth century in a new, superficial and popular form, namely in Wolff's dogmatic metaphysics. Here again we find, from the subjective side, a formalistic knowledge with its distinctions and external unifications, and, from the objective side, a multiplicity of dead substances, material and nonmaterial, complex and simple. Dogmatism asserted that this whole world of essences is fully *known* by reason. Kant proved that this world is also fully *posited* by reason, and he thereby destroyed it as a real world. But if the real side of the world created by rational dogmatism disappeared in Kant, its subjective side, the side of knowledge, remained as before. For, although Kant attempts to reduce all knowledge to a few basic forms, these forms are deprived of inner connection among themselves, and Kant uses them only as a general schema, not deriving real knowledge from them. This externality and immobility (*Starrheit*) of rational categories is conclusively removed in the dialectical self-development of the speculative concept—in Hegel's logical philosophy. The concept is self-differentiated and becomes its own opposite.[87] Instead of isolated hypostasized abstractions of reason we have the moving, living idea—the true form of that which actually exists. But Hegel could not recognize his idea as only the *form of that which exists*, since for him nothing *existed*. Indeed, in the earlier philosophy, that which exists appeared either in the form of the dead substances of dogmatism or in the form of the absolutely meaningless *Ding an sich* of critical philosophy. And, having legitimately rejected both the one and the other, Hegel, remaining on the ground of Western philosophy, had to reject in general all that exists as such. In this respect his philosophy is the most complete expression of the moment of negative reason or pure reflection. The pseudo-that-which-is of reason is rejected by the dialectical movement of the concept, and all reality thus passes to this dialectical movement, which, in fact, is what Hegel calls the speculative concept or the absolute idea. Thus, Hegel had to acknowledge that only the concept in itself has real being. Only the speculative concept is real—not as a thought in our head, and not as the objective form of that which exists, but in itself, as concept. But it is clear that the proposition *the concept is in itself* either does not consist of anything but words or contains the *hypostasization* of the concept. For if the speculative concept, taken purely logically, is the true, adequate form of that which exists, then, affirmed *separately* from its content, as existing in itself, this form is nothing else but a hypostasized abstraction. Having removed all the rational hypostases of the old metaphysics in his absolute idea, Hegel hypostasized this idea. And however far the great destroyer of all scholastic determinations may be from scholasticism, his own principle—the concept in itself—is nothing else but the scholastic *entitas*, substantial form, *universale ut reale*.

Hegel, rejecting all immediate content, considered only the formal or logical side to be real. Such a pronounced one-sidedness necessarily provoked, as we have already shown, a reaction in the opposite, just as one-sided, direction. Considering the absolute form of logical philosophy to be an empty abstraction, one began to search for a purely immediate, empirically given content, without understanding that content taken separately from its logical form is just as empty an abstraction, and to recognize it as that which truly exists is a similar hypostasization of an abstraction. Here, instead of hypostasized concepts, we have, at first, hypostasized elements of matter, material points, atoms, as the principles of empirical reality. But it is very obvious that the *material* atom is entirely reducible to formal, relative determinations, that the unknown principle of immediate independent reality, i.e., the principle of *action*, consists not in the atom as material element but in *force* (speaking the language of primitive innocence, the language of Dr. Buchner) which is inseparably connected with the atom. It is just as obvious that what, in external action or for another is force, in itself is *will*. Indeed, will is the inner principle of action and, therefore, of reality. And here Schopenhauer recognizes will as an independent first principle, as the unique really existent *Ding an sich*. But it is clear that will *in general*, will in itself, is a completely empty abstraction. Schopenhauer refers to immediate inner experience, in which we have will as reality. But, in inner experience, as we already mentioned in the second chapter, we only have will determined in a certain way, with a determinate object and character. But Schopenhauer's metaphysical will, will in itself without any determination, which we do not know and cannot know in immediate experience (since it does not exist at all outside of our abstraction), is only the *concept* of the first principle of reality *in general*, i.e., the first principle of reality *abstractly thought*, the direct counterpart of Hegel's absolute idea and the same sort of hypostasized abstraction as the latter. Hegel's logic is the development of the absolute ideal form, of those general categories that determine all that exists from the objective or for-mal side. This logical form is acknowledged by Hegel as reality in itself without that which is determined by it. That is, it is hypostasized. In Schopenhauer the opposite principle—the material principle by which all that exists is posited as such,[88] i.e., as reality—is taken just as abstractly. The principle of action, will, is taken by Schopenhauer just as abstractly, i.e., without any logical content, without any form,[89] as Hegel took form alone without any immediate reality determined by it. These two principles, taken in their exclusiveness, are equally abstract and untrue. The difference, however, is that the logical concept as such contains the moment of differentiation. There-fore from his principle Hegel could logically understand all the diverse forms of the existing world, whereas Schopenhauer's principle—will as such without any object, without any logical content—is absolutely indeterminate, a principle from which nothing can be derived ("The will as thing in itself is absolutely groundless," says Schopenhauer).[90]

If Schopenhauer had rigorously adhered to his concept of will as metaphysical entity, the transition from will to the world of forms would have been inconceivable, and philosophy would therefore have been inconceivable: Schopenhauer would have had nothing to say. But he *personifies* his metaphysical will and makes it into an acting and suffering subject. And all positive content is, of course, taken from limited, individual will. From this we get a constant *quid pro quo*: Schopenhauer speaks of his metaphysical will, but all that he says about it has meaning sole-ly with reference to the individual will of separate subjects, and precisely insofar as they are limited, insofar as their will cannot have metaphysical significance. All of the contradictions and alogisms in Schopenhauer's philosophy can be reduced to this basic misunderstanding. We shall show this with reference to the chief of these alogisms. We are considering Schopenhauer in

detail because the most immediate goal of our critical investigation—Hartmann's system—is only a complementary modification of Schopenhauer's philosophy.

According to Schopenhauer's doctrine the whole world of
forms, the world of representation, is only a phenomenon in the
mind, while the mind itself (*Intellekt*) is, as Schopenhauer
explains in detail, only a product of the will to life (*des Willens
zum Leben*), which creates this world as an auxiliary tool for its
goals, namely as a medium of motives (*Medium der Motiven*). As
a result, the mind originally has only a practical, not a theoretical function.[91] It is obvious that here one can take mind-producing will to mean only determinate, individual will, namely
the will of organic beings that need a medium of motives, for
will as *Ding an sich*, having nothing outside of itself, cannot have
any goals and even less can it need mind as the medium of
motives. However, in the general framework of Schopenhauer's
philosophy, one should understand the mind-producing will to
signify precisely the metaphysical will, for only it is the *prius* of
the mind, while the individual will, i.e., will as determined by
forms of representation, already presupposes the representing
mind and therefore cannot condition the mind's existence. In
order for will to become individual, to appear in the multiplicity of organic beings, it is already necessary to have the existence
of the representing mind, since only its forms (space, time, and
causality) posit real multiplicity or individual being. Thus,
Schopenhauer can derive mind only from metaphysical will,
which, however, does not contain any basis for this derivation,
being absolutely empty and indeterminate. Therefore, in
explaining the actual origin of the mind, Schopenhauer must
mean—instead of one indeterminate will—the multiplicity of
individuals with volition, existing really, which contradicts his
doctrine of the illusoriness, i.e., the exclusive phenomenality, of
individual being.

The second chief alogism of Schopenhauer's philosophy is his assertion that will as such suffers. Suffering in the objective or logical sense is the name given to the determination of one thing by some other thing, external to it. From the subjective or psychic side this corresponds to unpleasant or morbid sensations of any kind. But it is clear that will as such—an all-one substance, not having anything outside of itself—cannot be determined by anything external, and thus cannot suffer in the objective sense (or therefore in the psychic sense, since this is only the other side of the same thing). Therefore, all that Schopenhauer so eloquently says about the suffering of the will actually refers exclusively to the suffering of limited subjects with volition, insofar as they are limited. And in this sense all that he says is perfectly true. Indeed, any separate being, any individual, in asserting its separateness and individuality, posits outside of itself the whole world, and the world relates to and acts upon this individual according to its own law, which is external to this individual and contradicts the inner tendency of the latter, while necessarily determining it, since this individual already bears within itself its own externality and limit—as its own body. Which is why every individual suffers

> The heart-ache and the thousand natural shocks,
> That flesh is heir to.[92]

Every individual being with volition inevitably suffers as a result of its real determination. That is an axiom. But the expression "will suffers" (unless it is taken figuratively) is completely absurd.

From the essential suffering of will follows the necessity of its self-negation. And here the very same contradiction appears. The question is asked: In the ascetic negation of the will to life, *who* is the subject of negation? According to Schopenhauer, will itself "is converted and negates itself." But since it is, in essence, only the willing of itself, only self-assertion (*Wille zum Leben*), how can will stop willing? That is, how can it lose its immediate nature? It is obvious that not will itself, but only the *willer* can stop willing. The subject of the negation of will is therefore the separate individual as such, i.e., precisely the personal being of the ascetic, insofar as he is a person, but not insofar as the metaphysical essence of will is manifested in him. For, under the latter presupposition, because of the unity and universality of metaphysical will, negation should have been expressed inseparably in all of its individual manifestations. But because some individuals negate the will to life while others affirm it, it is clear that this affirmation and negation belong not to an essence common to all individuals but to their personal individuality. But, according to Schopenhauer, no individuality (and consequently this goes for the person too) has independence; every individuality is only a phenomenon or appearance of the will to life. In Schopenhauer separate individuals have the same relation to the universal will as individual modes have to substance in Spinoza. But how can a transient phenomenon negate its eternal essence? What would Spinoza have said about a mode that destroys the substance? It is clear that universal, metaphysical will can as little be the *object* of negation as its *subject*. The real subject of negation is the *person* of the ascetic, while the real object of negation is his *personal, particular* will.

Hartmann attempts to remove the contradictions and one-sidedness of Schopenhauer's system, but he does this only by placing *next* to Schopenhauer's exclusive principle another principle, which is missing in Schopenhauer: idea or representation. But thought does not yet gain much from the fact that to one hypostasized abstraction is added another. In fact, in Hartmann, will *in itself* does not have any object, and idea *in itself* does not have any content. As such, both principles are only the possibility of will and representation. This empty possibility is affirmed by Hartmann as existing in itself, as preceding the actual being of the world. Will and representation, which are initially in a state of pure possibility, pass into actuality, posit the actual world and then, by means of the cosmic process, return to the former potentiality. Since only that can pass into another which itself exists (for that which does not exist cannot pass into anything), it is clear that Hartmann conceives will and representation as *existing* in a state of potentiality prior to their actual being. He conceives *pure potentiality as existing in itself separately from actuality*. That is, he hypostasizes the abstract concept of potentiality, despite the completely relative character of this concept. Indeed, logically, potentiality is always conceived only in relation to something other, actually existent, as *belonging* to this something other, in no wise by itself. Thus, for example, when we say that a seed is potentially a tree, or that a larva is potentially an insect, potentiality here is only an attribute (*accidens*) of an actual being—of a seed or a larva. A larva is the potentiality of an insect. Clearly, the extremely simple truth here is that a larva has the possibility or capability of becoming an insect. The same thing that, as an insect, is only a potentiality is, as a larva, a completely actual being, in relation to which something else, for example, an egg, is only a potentiality. In general, *possibility* is necessarily conceived as belonging to that which "can"; pure possibility, however, i.e., possibility by itself, is equivalent, as even Hartmann acknowledges, to pure nonbeing. But to consider pure nonbeing as existing and acting is the height of absurdity.

To justify this absurdity Hartmann could not, of course, refer to Plato, who recognized the nonexistent (*mē on*) as existing in a certain sense. For Plato (together with Heraclitus) means by this only the indisputable truth that all relative, finite being equally participates (*metechei*) in being and nonbeing. Thus, in his brilliant dialogue *The Sophist*, the Eleatic guest says:

> It follows that there is nonbeing both in movement and in all kinds of things. In all these things the nature of the

> other makes each of them other than being, i.e., non-
> being. We are therefore right in saying that all of them,
> taken together, are nonbeing in this respect, and, con-
> versely, because they participate in being, we refer to them
> as being and call them beings. . . . When we speak of non-
> being, this evidently is not something that is contrary to
> being, but is something other.[93]

Plato's *mē on* has the same meaning as Aristotle's *dunamis*, which is nothing else but relative nonbeing (and thus relative being). According to Aristotle, all that exists, except the pure entelechy (*actus purus*) of God, is partly act (*energeia*) and partly potentiality (or matter: *dunamis = hule*). And one and the same thing is actuality with respect to what is lower than it and potentiality with respect to what is higher, and vice versa. Taking Plato and Aristotle as his point of departure, Schelling in his final system places a great importance on the difference between absolute being (*ouk on*) and only relative nonbeing (*mē on*), to which potentiality or possibility belongs. But, in Schelling, possibility is a concept, a thought existing in a thinking reason. Hartmann's primordial potentiality, however, is not a thought, for there is no thinker. But it is also not something objectively actual, for all actuality has yet to issue forth from it. This potentiality is therefore pure, absolute nonbeing, and Hartmann hypostasizes this pure negation as the absolute first principle.

What has been said is sufficient to allow one to see to what extent the doctrine of Schopenhauer and Hartmann shares the general limitation of Western philosophy: the one-sided dominance of rational analysis, which affirms abstract concepts in their separateness and therefore necessarily hypostasizes them. Having shown this negative side in the philosophy of will and representation, we must now clarify its positive significance in the historical development of consciousness.

Chapter IV

Having shown the general course of philosophical thought before Schopenhauer, having expounded the systems of Schopenhauer and Hartmann and indicated the formal limits of these systems—limits that they share with all of Western philosophy and that consist in the constant hypostasization of relative, abstract concepts—I must now try to arrive at my real destination: the explanation of the essential significance of the "philosophy of the unconscious" in that centuries-old intellectual development of the West whose final crisis is expressed in this philosophy. But to do that, I must yet consider for a while the philosophical doctrine that constitutes both the turning point and the link between two periods of Western philosophy: I mean Hegel's system, which, by concluding philosophical rationalism and expressing it in all its exclusiveness (and thus making its limitations obvious), called into being the demand for another philosophy, not abstract–logical, but positive[94]—a demand which the "philosophy of the unconscious" is trying to satisfy. Thus, let us return to Hegel.

The essence of Hegel's philosophy consists in the assertion that true knowledge does not have any object outside of itself, that knowledge contains within itself its own object, and is therefore absolute knowledge. Hegel says:

> In absolute knowledge the separation between object and self-consciousness (*Gewissheit seiner selbst*) is completely removed, and (objective) truth has become equivalent to this self-consciousness (*dieser Gewissheit*), just as this self-consciousness has become equivalent to truth. Thus, pure science presupposes liberation from the opposition of consciousness (*Gegensatz des Bewusstseyns*). Pure science contains *thought* insofar as thought is precisely also the thing *in itself*, or the thing in itself insofar as the latter is also pure thought. As science, truth is a developing self-consciousness and has the peculiarity that that which exists in and for itself is the known concept, while the concept as such is that which exists in and for itself.... It is this objective thinking that is precisely the content of pure science.[95]

Ordinary knowledge is understood as a relationship between the knower and the object, which abide independently of each other, and is therefore only an abstract unity. This externality is removed in Hegel's logic:

> Logic has been defined as a science of pure thought, having pure knowledge as its principle—not an abstract unity but a living, concrete one, because here (in logic) the opposition existing in the consciousness between the subject existent for itself and another such existent, an objective one, is overcome, and being is recognized as the pure concept in itself, and the pure concept is recognized as true being.[96]

When an external object is presupposed in knowledge, knowledge clearly cannot be free and independent but is always conditioned by empirical externality. Even if certain *a priori* knowledge has been admitted, it has only had an exclusively formal significance, as completely empty in itself and receiving all of its content from outside, from the empirical domain (that is how it is in Kant). If, on the contrary, knowledge does not have an external object, it must obviously receive its content from itself, must *create* it itself. Thus, instead of knowledge which consists of separate, formal, mutually external, fixed categories, appended to empirical content, a free knowledge must appear, self-developing, i.e., deriving all of its own content from its own principles, without any external relation:

> Form purified in thought (i.e., a logical concept liberated both from external objects and from the subjective finiteness of *I*, the separate consciousness) contains within its own self the capacity to *determine* itself, i.e., to give itself a *content*, and to do this in its necessity, as a system of thought determinations (*Denkbestimmungen*).[97]

Logical knowledge is capable of such inner self-development because every determinate concept is clearly *relative*, i.e., contains within itself the necessity of its own opposite or its own *negation*. But this negation, as the negation of a *determinate* concept, is already something positive:

> The sole knowledge necessary for achieving the scientific process (and it is essential that we try to acquire a simple understanding of this knowledge) is knowledge of the logical law that all that is negative has a uniformly positive significance, or that what contradicts itself is resolved not into zero, not into an abstract nothing, but essentially only into the negation of its own *particular* content, or that such negation is not total negation but only *negation* of that *determinate object* which is resolved, and therefore it is *determinate* negation. The result thus essentially contains that from which it proceeds. Strictly speaking, this is a tautology, for otherwise it would be something immediate, not a result. Insofar as that which results (*das Resultirende*), negation, is a *determinate* negation, it has *content*. It is a new concept, but a higher, richer concept than the preceding one, for it has been enriched with the negation of the preceding concept, or with its opposite. The new concept

contains the preceding concept, but also more than it. The new concept is the unity of the preceding concept and its opposite. In this way the system of concepts must, in general, be formed, and—in a continuous, pure progress, borrowing nothing from outside—attain its completion.[98]

Since the content of knowledge is wholly produced by the inner development of logical concepts, it is clear that this knowledge and development can *begin* only from a concept that does not have any content, from an absolutely indeterminate concept, which presupposes nothing, i.e., from a concept as *pure being*. This being, as not having any content, as a perfect void, is clearly pure *nothing*. Pure being thus becomes its own opposite, passes into it, which gives us the new concept of *becoming (das Werden)*. This concept is no longer an absolute abstraction, like the previous one, for in it two opposite moments (being and nothing) are united:

> Every time one speaks of being and nothing, this third thing (*das Werden*) must be presupposed, for they do not exist by themselves, but are only in becoming, in this third thing. But this third thing has many empirical forms, which are removed or neglected by abstraction in order that its products—being and nothing—be retained each by itself and be protected from transition.[99]

If the first two abstract concepts thus do not have any reality in themselves, but have reality only in the third thing, then it is necessary to say about this third thing that it too, *in itself*, has no reality. Rather, it receives reality from the following, more concrete, concept and so on, to the end. Indeed, it is obvious that if *being in general* does not really exist, neither does becoming or transition *in general*. Only a *determinate* transition exists, so that this concept requires for its reality the concept of *determinate being (das Daseyn)*. But, again, determinate being in general (*Daseyn uberhaupt*) does not exist: it must be determined *in one way* and *another*, it must be *this* thing and *another*, etc. All logical development consists in the fact that a certain concept as abstract cannot be real in itself, but can be real only in another, more concrete, concept. But the latter too is not real in itself, i.e., its concreteness is only relative and therefore requires yet another concept, etc.

> Consciousness can, of course, make, for example, empty space, empty time, itself as empty consciousness, or pure being its object and content. However, consciousness does not remain there but propels itself, hurries (*drangt sich*) from that emptiness to what is better, i.e., to a content that is most concrete in some way. And however bad this content may be, it is, as concrete, nevertheless better and truer.[100]

In general, "against the simple action of abstraction it is necessary also to simply indicate empirical existence, in which alone that same abstraction is something, has being."[101]

Thus, an abstract concept (and all the moments of logic, including the last, the absolute idea, are abstract concepts) cannot, as abstract, have independent reality. An abstract concept must necessarily be *in another*. It must possess a certain empirical substratum, whose actual existence is not posited, is not produced by the logical concept. For, to produce its own substratum, the logical concept must already exist in itself in its abstractness, but that is obviously impossible. Thus, if, as Hegel asserts, a logical concept, by its own inner development, produces its own content, this content does not *exist actually*, but is only *thinkable*. That is, all logical concepts are only general *possibilities* of being, from which, in themselves, no actual existence yet follows.

I will illustrate this with a common example. We have a certain concept of a triangle, necessitating that the sum of its three angles be equal to two right angles. All other theorems concerning the triangle can be derived from the concept or definition of the latter, in a manner similar to that by which Hegel, from the concept of pure being, derives the remaining logical moments. But it is clear that neither in the concept of the triangle nor in the necessary properties that logically follow from this concept is any actual existence affirmed, is it affirmed that any triangles exist actually, i.e., outside of our thought. One can say using Hegel's language that the concept of the triangle produces its own content, but this content is only thinkable or possible, not actual. From this concept, i.e., from this *thought* of mine, the only thing that follows is that the triangle is *possible*, for in the contrary case I could not think it, just as I cannot think, for example, a circular square (unthinkability = impossibility). Furthermore, the properties that logically follow from the concept of the triangle constitute the *necessary conditions* for the existence of any triangle (i.e., if any exists). *If* any triangle actually exists, the sum of its angles must equal two right angles. But even if no triangle actually existed, the concept of the triangle with all of its properties would obviously not thereby change in any way. Thus, the *concept* of the triangle is only the *possibility* of a triangle. But precisely the same thing is applicable to all concepts. Thus, if from Hegel's logic we take some more general concept, for example, the concept of *being-for-itself* (*Für-sich-seyn*), it is clear that we do not find out from this concept whether or not anything that is for itself actually exists. We can discover this only empirically. On the basis of the concept we can assert only that being-for-itself is *thinkable* or *possible*, and that, *if* something that exists for itself actually exists, it must satisfy all the logical moments that are contained in the concept of being-for-itself. However, in general, in logical concepts we know only the possibilities and necessary[102] conditions of that which exists, not that which exists itself.

The abstractness and, therefore, the nonactuality of logical concepts is involuntarily recognized by Hegel himself, when, contradicting his own basic principle, to logic (the science of pure concepts) he adds the philosophy of nature and the spirit, when he supplements the sphere of the absolute idea with the spheres—having equal rights—of external things and the self-conscious subject. According to his assertion, the logical idea is *actualized* in nature and the human spirit. But here, as in everything that Hegel says about the relation of idea to nature and spirit, there appears that indeterminacy and fogginess of metaphorical expressions which Schelling, in his positive philosophy, was the first to notice and ridicule. Indeed, what does the phrase "the logical idea is actualized in nature" mean? Some of Hegel's disciples (for instance, Rosenkranz), taking as their point of departure many expressions of the teacher himself, take this actualization to mean that the idea passes into, emanates into nature or *posits* nature, so that the logical idea appears here in the form of the absolute spirit or God. Even though such an explanation (which is intrinsically absurd, for it involves the hypostasization of an abstract concept) does not, in general, contradict the view of Hegel (who, himself, constantly personifies the idea), it does not conform to the obvious truth, expressed several times by Hegel himself, that the pure concept is only the *logical prius* of nature, but does not have an *actuality* separate from nature, does not exist in its abstractness, and therefore cannot pass into nature or produce it.

But, if this is the case, logical concepts are only general forms of natural being, abstracted and posited in themselves by our *reason*. Thus, in their universality, in their purely logical being, logical concepts exist only for us, as abstractions of our rational thought. This uniquely rational outcome of Hegel's philosophy, expressed by so-called left Hegelians, is obviously a self-negation of this philosophy. The logical concept, which first was an absolute principle, appears here as something conditioned and subjective. Through the recognition that actuality does not belong to the logical concept, the *limits* of logical philosophy as exclusively *formal* are recognized, and the question arises: What does actuality consist in? Or, using the most general expression: What is that substratum or that matter whose general forms are expressed in logical concepts?

The limits of the philosophical development that reached its culmination in Hegel's system are also disclosed from another side, from the subjective side. The subject of philosophy, as of all scientific knowledge, is a *separate individual as a thinking individual*. But thinking and knowledge have a close inner connection with another side of man's being, namely with *will* as the principle of action and active (practical) life. This connection already consists directly in the nature of both the one and the other, insofar as, on the one hand, all knowledge is produced by the striving for, or the will to, knowledge, while, on the other hand, all will or every volition has its object as a representable object, i.e., as knowledge. But besides this immediate connection between knowledge and will in general, there is a particular connection between properly human knowledge and will, insofar as human activity ceases to be determined exclusively by the instinctive volitions of sensuous nature, to which, from the cognitive side, there correspond immediate sensuous perception and elementary single acts of judgment and conclusion. Because of the complex social life of human beings, their activity cannot be determined exclusively by mere volitions and representations of instinct, which, though containing the root of the common, generic life of human beings, is sufficient, in its immediately physical character, only on the first, elementary levels of social life—in the family, in the life of race or tribe. With the growth and development of the social organism the connection of common physical origin among its members becomes more and more distant, the instinct of kinship is gradually weakened. And what is therefore necessary for the further existence of society is another connection, ideal but just as real, that would communicate a new strength to the physical connection, a connection that, by itself, is insufficient. Such an inner ideal connection presupposes universal or rational thought, i.e., a thought which, transcending immediate representation and particular thought acts, forms a general ideal view and, resolving in this view the higher theoretical questions, at the same time gives absolute principles and norms for the practical social life of human beings.

It is clear that, if this ideal view is to directly possess universally obligatory binding power, to have a greater power over the minds and wills of people than physical instinct, it cannot be a product of the clear discursive thought of separate individuals, cannot be a result of analytical knowledge. Rather, it must be a conviction based on the unconscious activity of reason, on faith and tradition, inseparably belonging to a whole nation or tribe. And, in fact, we see that the primordially general ideal view has exclusively such a character—the character of *religion*. *Philosophical* views, on the other hand, as products of personal thought, arise only with the specialized development of *personality*, when separate individuals acquire total inner independence, begin to live *for themselves*, and, with a clear consciousness, independently pose questions for themselves and resolve them through their own personal understanding independently of the common national thought and a world-view based on the latter. In other words, philosophy appears only when the former social organism begins to decompose. Rooted in this way in the split between the individual and *society*, philosophy is therefore the beginning of the split between *theory* and *practice*, between *school* and *life*. Indeed, in the theoretical domain, the thought of the philosopher has all its actual significance and complete independence. Here the thinker is the all-powerful lord and master: the deed is done as soon as the thought is expressed, for here thought is deed, is everything. Completely natural is the desire of philosophers that their thought become the thought of all others, that the theoretical truth recognized by them become universally recognized, but even if this does not happen, the *theoretical* truth does not thereby lose anything (Galileo's famous aside: "Nonetheless, it does move!"). Philosophers who enter upon the practical domain find themselves in a completely different situation, if here too, in questions of life, they wish to act like philosophers, i.e., to establish general principles and norms of activity, ideals of the social order.

Clearly, to express these principles and ideals is not enough; it is also necessary to translate them into reality. Without that they would have no meaning: a *practical* truth that remains only in the domain of theory is a contradiction. However, it is not in the power of philosophers to realize their moral ideals. Practical questions are a matter of personal interest for all; their resolution depends on the general will, and philosophers are therefore powerless here against the national majority. In order to do anything, they must first instill their principles in the minds and wills of this majority, and for that they have to uproot the former beliefs of the nation that are not in agreement with their views. This is made more difficult by the fact that these beliefs have long been part of life, that they have found expression in certain social forms that are powerful in their factual significance and in their authority rooted in age-hallowed tradition. Against these forms philosophical conviction alone is an insufficiently powerful weapon. Impossible for philosophical thought is the double victory over the national faith and over the social order conditioned by this faith. It is impossible as long as this faith is powerful and this order is strong, and philosophical thought cannot weaken them by direct action. They are weakened only after many centuries of historical development. Until then philosophers, if they do not wish to be dreamers and utopians, must completely renounce practical tasks, must completely detach themselves from the national faith and national life, and turn their activity exclusively toward theoretical questions. They must have as their object that which exists only insofar as it is known by *thought*, and not insofar as it is produced by *will*. Thus, if at the beginning the impotence of philosophical consciousness with respect to the will of the masses naturally forces philosophy to refrain from the questions of life, afterwards it is the purely theoretical nature of the tasks resolved by philosophy, its abstract character, that deprives it of the possibility of having any significance in the practical domain, any influence on the national life.

From its very beginnings up to our own time, Western philosophy has found itself precisely in such a situation. In the Middle Ages spiritual life for the national majority was completely determined by a world-view based on Christian faith in the form of Catholicism. This world-view gave higher goals for the will and ideal norms for activity, and thus determined all of moral life. Embodied in the Roman church, this view indisputably also had a determining significance for social life. Christian faith had an absolute significance for the general consciousness; this consciousness could not question the truth or rationality of this faith. However, medieval philosophy poses precisely this question. Thus, the task of medieval philosophy (i.e., the task of reconciling faith with reason or of justifying faith before the court of reason) was not the task of the common national consciousness. This consciousness did not need such a reconciliation; that was the task solely of the individual, personal mind. Medieval philosophy, which posed and solved this problem, confined itself to the scholastic approach and therefore is very justly called scholasticism. Thus, the split, the external relation, between faith and knowledge was expressed in the split, in the external relation, between life and science—in the *scholastic* character of science.

This scholastic character was retained by the new philosophy. It was impossible for this philosophy to have a practical significance because of its task, which consisted in determining the general, basic principles of that which is, of the eternal nature of things and the relation of this eternal nature to the subject as knower. Substantial being outside the knowing subject is first presupposed, and, as a result of development (in German idealism), the eternal nature of things is recognized as being identical with the logical forms of our knowledge. Both this task and its completion clearly have an exclusively theoretical character, including only those questions which are posed by the subject as only a *knowing* subject, without any reference to the demands of the subject as a *willing* subject, without any reference to questions of will. Indeed, alongside the world of eternal and unchanging forms of objective being and knowledge, there exists another reality, changing and agitated: the subjective world of human will, activity, and life. Alongside the theoretical question *What exists?* we find the practical question *What should be?*, i.e., What should I desire? What should I do? What should I live for? To this question theoretical philosophy could not, by its nature, give any answer, while the last coryphaeus of this philosophy, Hegel, completely rejected this question, ridiculed it. All that is rational, he says, *exists*; therefore, *nothing should be*. To assume that truth, goodness, etc. need our personal activity for their realization is obviously to consider them ineffective and impotent; however, an ineffective truth is not a truth, but an empty, arbitrary fantasy. Such a view is completely necessary from the point of view of exclusively theoretical philosophy, but Hegel's argument is inconvenient in that it proves too much. In its negation it embraces (something which Hegel, of course, did not have in mind) all historical reality. What, in fact, is history if not the constant realization by human activity of that which at first is only a subjective, ineffective ideal? That which *exists* now was previously only something that *should* have been; what is actual now was only desired then; will passed into action, and action left material results. Thus, between that which is and that which should be, between the actual and the desired, between the world of knowledge and the world of desire, there is no absolute separation. One thing constantly passes into another. There is no boundary between them, and abstract philosophy, by asserting such a boundary, only asserts its own limit. Moral actuality is foreign to this philosophy only because all actuality is foreign to it, for, as we have seen, the result of this philosophy has been that, setting as its task the knowledge of that which actually is, it has in fact come to know only the possible or thinkable, i.e., the general forms of social being, the necessary conditions of actuality, not actuality itself.

However, precisely now, in the nineteenth century, the time has arrived for philosophy in the West to come out of its theoretical abstractness, its scholastic self-containment, and to assert its sovereign rights in the business of life. The common religious foundations of Western life, both private and social, have been shaken by the religious and political movements of the last three centuries. The old religious world-view has lost all real meaning for the majority of educated people. Or, in any case, it has ceased to be the supreme, determining principle in their consciousness. Meanwhile, in the masses, the religious world-view has been transformed into a lifeless superstition, based exclusively on everyday habit. Thus, with the weakening of the religious consciousness, it became necessary to seek the supreme, determining principles for life in the philosophical consciousness. This consciousness also had another reason for leaving its logical abstractness: namely, the purely theoretical development of philosophy had reached its final culmination in Hegel's system, and, as we have seen, it was impossible to go any further in this direction.

The result attained was the recognition of the absolute signif-icance of reason, i.e., of the human *I as knower*. The assertion of Hegel's philosophy that the essence of the all is a logical concept was equated, from the subjective side, with the assertion that the essence of the human *I* is logical *knowledge*, that the subject or person has significance only in knowledge, as a knower. But here too an exclusive assertion, by virtue of its exclusiveness, passes into its opposite. Indeed, if human knowledge is absolute in Hegel's sense, i.e., if it does not refer to anything that exists, does not have any content different from itself as form, it is clear that, in this knowledge, nothing is known. Knowledge becomes a purely *subjective* activity of the knower, to whom absolute signif-icance thus passes. Instead of the objective essences of the old metaphysics, the knowing *subject* is recognized as the sole actual existent. The leading role is played not by the logical idea but by that subject which knows it, to which it *belongs*. The *proper* essence of the subject is its *self-assertion* or will, that which is pre-eminently expressed in affects and desires. The root of all of sub-jective life, not excluding theoretical knowledge, is here, since reason is only an instrument for will. Thus, the supreme signifi-cance passes to *human beings* as such, i.e., in their subjective, per-sonal being. This transition *ad hominem* was (as is well known) effected in German philosophy by Feuerbach, a former disciple of Hegel. Feuerbach writes:

> Humanity's being is its *higher being*. Although religion calls the supreme being God and considers him an objective being, in truth this is only humanity's own being. There-fore, the turning point of universal history consists in the fact that, from now on, God for humanity must be not *God, but humanity*."[103]

Humanity's self-assertion is not, of course, the assertion only of its given being, *tou einai*; it is also *tou eu einai*, i.e., the *striving for happiness*. And if humanity's self-assertion is taken as the basis, human happiness will be the principle of morality, the supreme norm of activity. Human beings desire to be happy—that is the supreme law. Moreover, since humanity *as such* is taken as the basic principle, and to be a human being is a property that belongs *equally* to *all* people, it follows that *all* people have an *equal* right to happiness, for, in principle, there is no basis for inequality. However, the existing social forms reject this equal right, admitting the *inequality* of class, property, and state *positions*, as a result of which some individuals possess what others lack, and the minority possesses what the majority lacks. This conditions for the majority a smaller possibility of happiness than for the minority. Therefore, for the attainment of the supreme goal—human happiness—it is necessary to destroy these imperfect social forms and to replace them with new forms, which would give to all people the same possibility of being happy. Thus, the supreme goal can most precisely be defined as the realization of *universal welfare*, a goal which constitutes the principle of *socialism*.

But if *in abstracto* the supreme principle is the self-assertion of *humanity in general*, then, in practice, i.e., for *each separate individual*, it is this individual's *own* self-assertion. And if *in abstracto* the supreme goal is human happiness in general, the necessary condition for which is universal and absolute equality, then, in practice, for each separate individual the supreme goal is this individual's own happiness, this individual's personal good, for which social equality or inequality is intrinsically a matter of indifference. Indeed, "humanity in general" is obviously an abstraction, whose reality is represented by each individual, but what obviously has immediate significance for each individual is only this individual's own happiness, whereas the good of others is only relative, insofar as it enters into the conditions of this individual's own happiness. Translating the supreme practical law—"humanity desires happiness"—from abstract to living language, we have: I—a given person—desire *my own* happiness. Thus, the *anthropological* principle is clarified to be the *egoistic* principle. But this clarification is the self-negation of socialism, for, because of it, socialism, first of all, loses its universal significance. For if the striving toward the general welfare must be based on egoism, it does not have any meaning for all those whose egoism can best be satisfied under the existing social inequality, for those for whom this inequality is profitable, i.e., for all people of privileged classes. Secondly, although the egoism of the cheated majority must produce an aspiration to change the existing social forms, the goal of this aspiration is not to establish *universal* equality and welfare (egoism can have nothing to do with this), but to exploit this change for personal profit. Instead of an aspiration to the general good, we necessarily get the exclusive self-assertion of each separate individual at the expense of all others, the war of each individual against all.

Thus, socialism becomes an exclusive *individualism*, the best theoretical expression of which can one indisputably find in Max Stirner: "For myself I am everything, and do everything for my own sake."[104] The supreme thing is by no means "humanity," as Feuerbach, for example, asserts; the *I* is higher than man:

> The fact that we are people, this is the least important thing in us, and has significance only insofar as this is one of our properties, i.e., our own.[105]

> I am a human being and, at the same time, more than a human being, i.e., I am the subject of this my mere property (that of being a human being).[106]

> Thus, away with everything that is not fully *mine*! You think that my work must, at the least, be a "good work"? What is good, what is evil? I myself am my work, and I am neither good nor evil: neither has any meaning for me. My work is neither God's nor humanity's; it is not true, good, just, free, etc. But it is exclusively *mine*, and it is not universal, but *unique*, as I myself am. Besides me there is nothing for me![107]

Thus, after philosophical rationalism rejected all objective reality in *theory*, all the objective principles of morality are now being rejected in *practice*. The absolute, exclusive self-assertion of *I* becomes the unique principle of life. For myself I am a god; all has significance for me only as a means for me; I do not recognize a limit to my egoism in another person. The sole limit for me is the limit of my power:

> I derive all right and all justification from *myself*; I have a right to everything that is in my power.[108] . . . Right will be reduced into its nothingness when it is swallowed by *power*, i.e., when the meaning of 'strength before right' is understood. Then all right (*Recht*) will proclaim itself as privilege (*Vorrecht*), while privilege will proclaim itself as superiority (*Ubermacht*).[109]

But the necessary recognition of the limits of my power already contains the self-negation of this individualism. I am a god for myself, but this "for myself" transforms my godhood into a cruel irony:

> A great god is hidden in my breast;
> He agitates and troubles my soul—
> Inside me he rules fully,
> But in the outer world he can do nothing.[110]

In the outer world my godhood encounters a countless number of other gods, and for these gods it itself is only an external means. But let it be the case that I defeat all of these gods who are my rivals and force them to acknowledge my godhood. Even then this godhood would remain only subjective (in a subjectivity which others acknowledge and which, primordially, I acknowledge myself), whereas objectively I would nonetheless remain insignificant and powerless in the face of the immutable forces of the natural law of material being, external to me. Objective reality, having disappeared long ago for the logical concept, retains its practical meaning for living people, as the *necessity of physical suffering and death*. In the face of this external reality, which sooner or later will transform my godhood into a dish for worms (similar gods for themselves), my self-assertion is absolutely powerless.

The only means to protect my self-assertion against the natural law, my independence from this law, is suicide. But here self-assertion is equal to self-negation, and independence here is illusory, for I cannot annihilate myself with a single free act of my will. My decision is always physically conditioned, as is its execution. Thus, there is no way that I can realize my self-assertion; I must renounce it. But I cannot renounce it in favor of dead, blind material necessity. Resignation in the face of material force is unthinkable for me—a rational force.

The subordination to external material force is unbearable for the self-asserting *I*, but it is necessary for it precisely insofar as its standpoint is exclusively that of self-assertion. For, since for this standpoint all inner significance belongs to the particular, individual being of the subject, it is clear that universal being, the law of all, must appear to the self-asserting *I* as a completely alien, absolutely external necessity, against which it cannot struggle, but with which it also cannot be reconciled, for such a reconciliation would mean its annihilation.

The inner connection between practical individualism and theoretical materialism, deadly for both, is broken by the philosophical affirmation that matter is only a phenomenon. The force of the universal is not material and mechanical; it is essentially *will*. The universal is homogeneous with the particular; the *not-I* is essentially the same thing as *I*.

> You are following a false path!
> Do not think we are joking.
> Is not the kernel of nature
> In the hearts of human beings?[111]

The self-asserting personality must not subject itself to blind material force; its reconciliation with the universal is not its annihilation. This clarifies the enormous practical significance of the philosophy of will and representation. But the founder of this philosophy—Schopenhauer—naturally expressed the new principle in a one-sided and limited form. As though blinded by the light of the truth he had discovered, he could not clearly distinguish the logical content contained in it. Having affirmed that the essence of the all is will and that the particular is thus substantially identical with the universal, he stopped, without explaining the precise rational meaning of these propositions and without developing their necessary logical consequences. From this we get the oddity that Schopenhauer usually takes the *essential unity* of personal will with the world substance to be their *actual identity*, as a result of which in his moral philosophy, as we have seen, the self-renunciation of personal arbitrariness is the self-renunciation of the world will, which has no rational meaning. In metaphysics—because he asserts will completely abstractly, separately from representation and reason—will is a blind force for him, essentially not differing in any way from matter.

The principle of will clearly gets its necessary development only through the addition of the logical or ideal moment, when will is conceived not abstractly but as an actual will, i.e., with an objective content or idea. We find a transition to this in Hartmann's system. But because of the formal limitation (indicated in the previous section) of all Western philosophy, a limitation which Hartmann shares, both first principles—will and idea—despite their union, retain in Hartmann their abstractness and are asserted by themselves, so that their union is only a juxtaposition of two abstractions taken as something independently existing. It is clear that will in itself is recognized as absolutely irrational, while idea in itself is recognized as absolutely impotent, devoid of all activity. The principle of actuality according to Hartmann is exclusively will—an irrational principle. Actual being therefore constitutes the essential character of irrationality.

Actual being is that which should not be. All actual being is essentially suffering and woe, because it originates not from absolute reason or idea, which is completely passive according to Hartmann, but is posited by the meaningless transition of will from pure potentiality, or nonbeing, to act. If the primordial origin of existence itself is therefore an irrational fact, a pure accident (*Urzufall*), the rationality or goal-directedness of the cosmic process recognized by Hartmann has only a secondary and negative significance. This rationality consists in the gradual destruction of that which is posited by the primordial irrational act of will. Reason is emancipated from will through the formation of consciousness, and all that exists receives the possibility—through the negation of the will to life—of returning to the state of pure potentiality, or nonbeing, which constitutes the final goal of the cosmic process.

Thus, in this system the suffering and despair of a separate individual are removed from the suffering and despair of all that exists. Particular, individual suicide is replaced by universal, collective suicide. But this suicidal view is grounded only in that aspect of Hartmann's philosophy which constitutes its transitory limitation. However, the solid foundation of the superconscious or all-one spirit, built from indestructible empirical materials by the tool of powerful logic, demands better (in both the logical and the practical sense) conclusions than those which the founder himself wishes to base on it. And although the principle of the all-one spirit does contain grounds for a relative, practical pessimism, it contains neither a logical possibility nor practical motives for collective suicide. The explanation and proof of these assertions constitute the final task of the present inquiry. The completion of this task should eliminate from Hartmann's system the elements that are contrary to good sense, and show the true significance of the positive results that are now being achieved by philosophy.

Chapter V

Undertaking now to determine the positive results of the philosophy of the unconscious, or (what is the same thing) the positive results of the whole philosophical development up to this point, I will consider these results (in conformity with the ancient classification scheme of philosophy) first with reference to *dialectics* or the doctrine of *knowledge*,[112] then with reference to *metaphysics* or the doctrine of *that which is*, and finally with reference to *ethics* or the doctrine of *that which should be*.

A first, superficial analysis of the entire domain of that which is known reveals to us three basic sources of knowledge: (1) *inner experience*, in which we know our own subjective being in its actuality; (2) *external experience*, in which we know external being in its reality; (3) and *reasoning* (*ratiocinatio*), or purely logical knowledge, in which we do not know any reality or any actuality, but affirm only certain necessary conditions or laws of being. In considering the interrelationship of these kinds of knowledge, we find, in the first place, that purely logical knowledge and external experience do not exist separately from each other, but are always united, although to different degrees. Thus, there is no doubt that the purely empirical material, which consists of the sensations of the external senses, becomes empirical knowledge only when these sensations are objectified and combined according to certain general and necessary laws, so that even immediate external apprehension, in which we have not simple sensations but whole interconnected representations, is already a matter of speculation, although unconscious. As regards *scientific* external experience, i.e., so-called empirical science, there is no need to mention that speculation (and this on the level of conscious thought) plays the major role in this experience, for no scientific truth is given in immediate experience. (But, as we have just pointed out, this immediate experience itself is, in fact, a result of speculation.) But, if there is thus no pure empiricism, then, on the other hand, there is also no pure speculation. For if objective knowledge is formed by speculation, it follows that speculation gives form to objective knowledge. And, in abstraction from its empirical content, speculation represents only empty possibilities, as we showed at the beginning of the previous section.

This is indisputable for *logical categories* as *general conditions* of being. As regards abstract representations or *generic concepts*, it is clear that they, as a result of *abstraction*, presuppose empirical data, but in themselves they also represent only an empty possibility. Rational or logical knowledge has a similar relation to the data of *inner* experience. Like the elements of the external world, the elements of the inner world can be formed into *actual* knowledge only through certain logical conditions or laws. But it is just as clear that, here too, these conditions or laws do not, in themselves, yet give any actual knowledge. They represent only an empty possibility, which can be actualized only thanks to the immediate data of inner experience. The relation of logical knowledge to experience in the objective domain was sufficiently explained in the preceding chapter in connection with Hegel's philosophy. Here I will try to show the same relation, but in the domain of inner phenomena, with primary reference to the English school of empirical psychology.

Let us assume that there exists a certain psychological law according to which given inner states are united, under certain conditions, in a certain determinate manner. Locke's school asserts that we know this law exclusively empirically—only as a certain existing relation of phenomena. However, if this is actually a law, and not an accidental fact, it clearly cannot be limited solely to the *given* relation of succession and coexistence, for in this case we could assert this relation only for cases known in our experience, and would have no right to recognize it as the general law for *all* homogeneous cases that have ever been or will ever be. Even such an extreme empiricist as John Stuart Mill acknowledges that the law (i.e., a certain relation) of causality (in the sense that is ascribed to causality in this school) always expresses an absolutely constant or necessary condition. But if this connection were confined solely to *our actual* experience, we would clearly not have the right to go outside the limits of the given experience, which we do when we assert that a certain connection is absolutely constant, i.e., that it not only occurs in facts known to us from actual experience, but that it should also occur in *all* like cases. We can assert such an absolutely constant connection of two phenomena only if the necessity of another phenomenon is already contained in the very *being* or *concept* of the given phenomenon, i.e., in its *general* properties, abstracted from all external relations. In fact, two phenomena of the inner world exist for us, first of all, in given actual experiences, and, secondly, in a general abstract understanding of them. Likewise, their connection, too, appears to have a dual character. Now, if the *thinkable* connection of these phenomena were only an abstraction from their actual connection in the *given experiences*, it could clearly have meaning only for *those* given cases. For it is clear that abstraction from certain given experiences can guarantee only these given experiences, not every future experience. If we assume the existence of such a guarantee (as even the empiricists do), this indisputably proves that, although the general concepts of certain inner phenomena are, from the subjective side, only abstractions from the given reality of these phenomena, nevertheless, once this abstraction is effected, once general concepts exist, the general connection between them is already deduced by thought exclusively from general necessary properties, without any reference to any particular experiences whatever. This general connection therefore presents that character of universality and necessity which in fact belongs to the connection thought by us, whereas, in the opposite case, if this connection were obtained by us wholly from actual particular experiences, its recognition would be confined solely to those given experiences. However, this is not the case in fact. Let me elucidate this with an example.

There is no doubt that the basic factors of psychical phenomena—will and representation—are known to us only from the actual inner experience of given volitions and representations. If—*per impossibile*—there were no *given* volitions and representations in our inner reality, we could not know anything about will and representation *in general*. But once we have acquired these concepts by means of experience, the general connection between them, according to which to every actual volition there must correspond a certain representation as an object or goal of the volition, this necessary connection between will and representation is already deduced from their general concepts themselves or from their *essence*, completely independently of any particular experiences whatever. For if this general relation were only an abstraction from relations given in an actual particular experience, it would go no further than this particular experience. But in fact we assert to the contrary that—*always* and *everywhere*, in *all* entities without exception—will is *necessarily* united with representation. The contrary, we say, is *impossible*, because it contradicts the very *essence* or *concept* of will. Thus, a certain relation between the phenomena of inner experience is deduced by us from their general concept and therefore is asserted as universal and necessary. Of course, this relation is actualized only in the given phenomena, apart from which it is only an empty possibility. But, on the other hand, these given phenomena are *possible* only in the case of this logical relation, which therefore constitutes the *necessary condition* of their existence. It is clear that the logical connection between will and representation by no means determines the reality of these inner phenomena, just as the absolute truth that twice two is four by no means determines the reality of the things that are subject to these numbers. But as soon as will and representation really exist, the logical relation that links them is an absolute necessity for them. To suppose that in some particular case will is not united with representation is just as impossible as to suppose that, given the actual existence of the things being counted, twice two is not equal to four in some particular case.

This makes it clear that the relation of logical or *a priori* knowledge to immediate experience in the domain of inner or psychical phenomena is completely identical with the same relation in the domain of external or physical phenomena. In both places, general logical forms (being in themselves only empty possibilities), in the case of the existence of a reality that corresponds to them, represent this reality's necessary condition or *law*. If logical forms outside of reality are only a possibility, reality in itself outside of logical forms is an impossibility, and therefore does not exist at all. Thus, on the basis of what has been said, we must acknowledge that empirical knowledge (in both external and inner experience) and logical or *a priori* knowledge do not constitute two radically separate and independent domains of knowledge. They are necessary for each other, since empirical knowledge is possible only in the case of logical conditions, while logical knowledge is real only in the case of empirical content. But in order that this important truth (which requires the inseparable union of pure logic and empiricism, with the two having equal rights) could be recognized, it was necessary for these two fundamental elements of knowledge to be exhausted in their particular exclusiveness, as a result of which their one-sided limitation would become evident. In fact, we see two main tendencies in the development of Western philosophy: the *rationalistic* tendency, which derives all knowledge from general concepts, and the *empirical* tendency, which derives it exclusively from actual experience. As is well known, this opposition had been expressed already in medieval scholasticism, which was divided into *realism*, which recognized general concepts (*universalia*) as the expression of real being and therefore derived real knowledge from them; and *nominalism*, which saw in these general concepts nothing more than the results of our abstraction, conventional signs or merely names (*nomina*), while it recognized actual knowledge only in immediate perception. In modern philosophy *each* of these two tendencies passes through *three appropriate phases or moments* in its development. In the *rationalistic tendency* these three moments are expressed: (1) by the so-called *dogmatic metaphysics*, the main representatives of which were Descartes, Spinoza, and Leibniz, together with Wolff. The essence of this first moment in the epistemological respect consists in the unconscious identification of thought with real being, i.e., being that is independent of our thought. For here it is presupposed that in the general concepts proper to our mind we think real independent essences, so that true knowledge is obtained from these primordial concepts (*ideae innatae, veritates aeternae*) and therefore in an *a priori* manner. Independent being, external to our thought, is presupposed in this moment. But this being is asserted unconsciously as perfectly corresponding to our thought of it: thought and being rest here in undifferentiated unity. (2) With the beginning of differentiation or distinct analysis there comes the necessary consciousness that, if our knowledge is *a priori*, i.e., if it has as its source exclusively our own subjective thought, we cannot know anything about that which is found *outside of our* consciousness, and that, consequently, if there is an independent essence, it is absolutely unknowable for us; and we know only *phenomena* in our *subjective* consciousness, determined by its general forms. Such is the result of Kant's *critique of reason*, which expresses this second principal moment of philosophical rationalism. But if all that we know does not transcend the bounds of our consciousness, the very difference between that which exists independently and phenomena, between that which is *in itself* and that which is *for us*, is then a difference in our consciousness, and the very concept of that which exists in itself is only a concept of our reason. Therefore, (3) everything is *concepts of our reason,* and reason is thus liberated from its subjective character; it becomes *universal* reason, and the contradiction between subjective thought and objective being is removed in the absolute identity of the absolute idea. This third and final moment of rationalism, expressed, as is well known, in Hegel's philosophy, is thus a return to the first moment, but now at the level of full consciousness. The mutual relation of these three phases in the development of rationalism can be expressed as follows:

1. (*Major* of dogmatism): That which truly is, is known in *a priori* knowledge.

2. (*Minor* of Kant): But in *a priori* knowledge, only the forms of our thought are known.

3. (*Conclusio* of Hegel): *Ergo*, the forms of our thought are that which truly is.

Or:

1. We think that which is.
2. But we think only concepts.
3. Ergo, that which is, is a concept.

The *empirical tendency* presents a similar course of development. Based on Bacon's philosophy, this tendency (1) affirms real experience as the sole source of knowledge and initially presupposes that, in this real experience, in empirical data, we know the true nature of the being that is external to us. That is the situation in Bacon and, in part, in Hobbes. (2) It is clear, however, that, if the sole source of our knowledge of the external world is *our* real experience, we know this world only to the extent that it acts upon us or relates to us by means of our external senses. For, in the contrary case, we would have to have preliminary concepts or innate ideas about the external world, but the existence of such ideas is refuted by the analysis of empiricism. It is true that our knowledge is composed of sense data processed by reflection (Locke). But this reflection, consisting of operations of our mind, evidently has only a subjective significance. Thus, data of the external senses are the primary source of our knowledge of the external world. But everything that is given by the external senses consists in various sensations, and sensations are states of our subjective consciousness. Therefore what we call external things, being wholly formed from our sensations, are only *representations* or ideas in *our spirit* (Berkeley). (3) But if the sole source of our knowledge is our real experience, we cannot recognize either external things or our spirit as having independence or substantiality, for in real experience we find spirit not in this experience itself as substance, but only in different *empirical states of consciousness*, to which all reality thus passes. This final stage of empiricism had already been expressed by Hume, and in recent times it has been expressed by John Stuart Mill, whose system of logic, although it is devoid of philosophical creativity, nevertheless in the consistency, clarity, and fullness with which it develops the empirical principle, has for this tendency approximately the same significance that Hegel's logic has for the rationalistic tendency.

The interrelationship of the stages in the development of empiricism can be expressed in the following syllogism:

1. (*Major* of Bacon). That which truly is, is known in our actual experience.

2. (*Minor* of Locke et al.). But in our real experience only different empirical states of consciousness are known.

3. (*Conclusio* of Mill). *Ergo*, the different empirical states of consciousness are that which truly is.

From this one can see that the extreme conclusions of the two opposite tendencies—rationalistic and empirical—have come together at one essential point, namely in the fact that both equally negate the proper being, both of what is known and of the knower, transferring the whole truth to the very *act of knowledge*. Exclusive rationalism and exclusive empiricism thus enter as two aspects into the single generic concept of *formalism*, for if neither the knower nor what is known exist, only the *form* of knowledge remains. The difference between Hegel's logic and Mill's logic in this respect consists only in the fact that, in Hegel, the primacy in real knowledge belongs to general logical concepts, from which, among other things, sensuous knowledge is already derived. In Mill, on the contrary, the sensuous states of consciousness are judged to be primary, and it is from these states that the higher logical ideas issue forth through abstraction. If rationalism cannot escape the vicious circle of general concepts and attain particular reality, empiricism, on the contrary, limited to particular data of phenomenal reality, can, remaining true in itself, by no means attain the universal and immutable laws necessary for true knowledge. As we have seen, the logical and empirical elements are equally necessary for true knowledge. And the exclusive isolation of one or the other element is therefore a one-sided *abstraction*, so that the limitation common to these two tendencies can be more closely defined in the concept of *abstract formalism*.

We find, for the first time, the appropriate synthesis of the logical and empirical elements in Hartmann's philosophy of the unconscious. Schopenhauer's philosophy of will and representation already contains these two elements, but not in an adequate relation. Recognizing as genuinely existing only what is known in immediate inner experience, i.e., *will*, Schopenhauer shifted the whole content of logical knowledge to the side of subjective representation. This brought him to obvious absurdities, which, as we have seen, he could avoid in part only by contradicting his own first principles. However, in Hartmann logic and empiricism have equal rights: he derives all knowledge from empiricism, but from an empiricism conditioned by logical thought. His slogan is: "Speculative results according to the inductive natural-scientific method." But it is obvious that no speculative results can be obtained from pure empiricism as it is understood, for instance, by the English school, i.e., from an investigation of the given reality, of particular facts, taken in their empirical particularity as the first principle. It is obvious that, from such an investigation, however exact and subtle it might be, one can obtain only particular results, which have significance only for that given reality which was subject to our actual investigation. In this manner we can find that, in such-and-such cases upon which our observation has focused, this and that occurred, such-and-such phenomena were found (both in direct observation and by means of experiments and analysis) in such-and-such interrelationships. That is all. In this manner we can find no universal and immutable laws that the unconscious empiricists so glory in, for any given reality guarantees only itself.

It is clear that empiricism does not possess that magical word (*logos*) which can transform particular and accidental facts into universal and necessary truths. What is necessary for this transformation is that logical thought, which transfigures the data of immediate experience, already has in itself the character of universality and necessity and contain the inevitable conditions or universal laws of reality. In recognizing this, Hartmann finds himself in agreement with the truth of rationalism. But on the other hand he avoids the exclusive assertion of rationalism that the logical concept is not only the law of reality but also integral reality itself, not only conditions real existence but also produces it out of itself. Hartmann, on the contrary, knows very well that the law of that which is, is just as negligible without this "that which is" whose law it is as this "that which is" is impossible without its logical condition. Therefore, all those logical conclusions to which Hartmann himself attaches firm meaning[113] are based on indubitable data of real experience and only thanks to this become actual truths, and not only empty possibilities. That is all that can be said about the epistemological aspect of the philosophy of the unconscious, because, although in the main (inductive) part of this philosophy we find an application of the true philosophical method, nevertheless the principle of this method, its general theoretical foundations, i.e., precisely that which constitutes epistemology or the theory of knowledge, is insufficiently clarified by Hartmann. And this insufficiency is also reflected in his *metaphysics*.

Since that which truly is—the object of metaphysics—obviously has being for us only through our knowledge (this is a tautology), it is clear that the relation of a philosophical tendency to metaphysics is wholly determined by its theory of knowledge, by the logic or epistemology of this tendency. Therefore, we can say *a priori* that those two one-sided tendencies of Western philosophy which, in the epistemological respect, are characterized as rationalism and empiricism, have a purely negative relation to metaphysics. Precisely in their logic they both equally reject the very possibility of metaphysics. And, in the first place, since in its final stage rationalism comes to the absolute identification of being with knowledge, to the assertion that that which is gets its true being only in our knowledge of it, it is clear that this completely annuls metaphysics as the doctrine of *that which is in itself*, in contradistinction to logic, as the doctrine of *our knowledge*. Indeed, the negation of an independent metaphysics, its complete absorption by logic, constitutes, as is well known, the distinctive feature of consistent rationalism, i.e., Hegelianism. On the other hand, empiricism, recognizing our experience as the sole source of knowledge, an experience in which we find only the states of our own consciousness, thereby denies the possibility of metaphysics as knowledge of that which is in itself. And empiricism either does not go beyond this denial of metaphysical *knowledge*, though it does acknowledge that the object of metaphysics, i.e., that which is in itself, has real *being*, and affirms only the absolute *unknowability* of that which is in itself, which is thus taken as the pure X (such a transitional view—to which in rationalism Kant's critical philosophy corresponds—is represented in the empirical tendency by the French positivists and, among the English, by Herbert Spencer, for instance). Or when the empirical principle is accepted with total consistency, the recognition of the very *existence* of metaphysical essence is removed. For if, in accordance with the principle of empiricism, all real knowledge is obtained from the given experience, all concepts to which nothing in this experience corresponds are either fictions or empty abstractions. And such precisely is that which is in itself, for we do not have anything like it in actual experience. This definitive empiricism (toward which John Stuart Mill, for example, tends), like Hegel's definitive rationalism, denies metaphysics because here the very object of metaphysics is reduced to zero. In Mill, metaphysics disappears in empirical psychology, while in Hegel it disappears in absolute logic.

It must be noted, however, that even if rationalism and empiricism, entering into the reason of their basic principles, reject all metaphysics together with its object, nevertheless, at the first, unconscious stages of their development both of these tendencies naturally produce metaphysical systems appropriate to them. These systems, both distinguished by an immaturity of thought, are *abstract spiritualism* in the rationalistic tendency and *materialism* in the empirical tendency. As regards the former, examples of which in the modern philosophy one can find in Descartes or in Wolff, its essence consists in the fact that, on the one hand, the absolute first principle is entirely reduced to abstract logical determinations. Since, however, the purely logical significance of these determinations is not yet consciously assimilated, then, on the other hand, to the first principle that they compose is attributed an autonomous existence independent of our thought, in the form of the absolute substance, the supreme monad, the receptacle of all reality (*Inbegriff aller Realität*), etc. This is the basis of that empty *deism* on which, even up to now, popular philosophy and liberal theology in France, England, and America subsist.[114] By contrast, the essence of *materialism* consists in the fact that, on the one hand, something empirically given (matter) is taken as the real first principle. But since the purely empirical significance of this given is not yet consciously assimilated, on the other hand, this empirical matter has ascribed to it the significance of the absolute and universal essence, which already transcends the bounds of the empirical, which has to do only with the given particular reality and by no means with universal essences. And since materialists do not give themselves any accounting of this transcending beyond the empirical, but rather imagine that they find themselves on solid empirical ground, materialism may justly be called *the unconscious metaphysics of empiricism*. If abstract spiritualism thus unconsciously betrays the rationalist principle by isolating its own absolute logical substance and attributing real, i.e., empirical, existence to this substance, then materialism betrays the empirical principle (just as unconsciously) by generalizing its own real empirical object (matter) and attributing to it universal and necessary, i.e., logical, significance. In other words, abstract spiritualism transcends the general logical concept into the domain of particular empirical reality, for it places its absolute essence outside of other essences, alongside them, and therefore as particular. By contrast, materialism[115] transcends the particular empirical reality into the domain of the general logical concept. The recognition that these metaphysical systems are based on such an unconscious transcending of lawful bounds necessarily leads to the negation of these systems, and, as a final result, as we have seen, both tendencies arrive at the denial of the very object of metaphysics.

Even though both of these unconscious metaphysics undoubtedly are made impossible through further philosophical development, this does not pertain to metaphysics in general in the sense of knowledge of that which truly is—in contrast to our given subjective knowledge, both abstract–logical and sensuous–empirical. We have seen that the rejection of metaphysics which characterizes both of these tendencies of Western philosophy has its origin in the intrinsic limits or one-sidedness of these tendencies. Therefore, philosophical doctrines which attempt to remove these limits necessarily restore metaphysics (in the sense noted), as we see in Schopenhauer's system, and especially in Hartmann's system. If, in fact, neither pure empiricism nor pure thought can take us out of the subjective sphere, the true synthetic method of philosophy (the first significant application of which we find in Hartmann) is that which is based on the recognition that, although all of our real knowledge comes from experience, this very experience already presupposes universal logical forms as a condition of its own possibility. These forms, however, are by no means subjective, for in our subjective thought which isolates them they are only abstract concepts, empty possibilities, and have actual being only in their concreteness, which is *independent of us* and endowed with empirical existence.

The union of the logical and empirical elements is thus by no means produced by our subjective knowledge (as Kant asserted in his "*a priori* synthesis"), but, on the contrary, is prior to our consciousness and is presupposed by the latter. This affirms that, in our knowledge, we refer to what exists independently, which in fact posits the possibility of metaphysics. On the other hand, it is no longer recognized (as it was in the old dogmatic metaphysics) that that which truly is abides in itself as an independent entity outside the knower (in which case metaphysical knowledge would be impossible, as was indeed proved by the Kantian criticism). On the contrary, an essential identity between metaphysical essence and the knower, i.e., our spirit, is presupposed. This essence is thus determined to be the *all-one spirit*, of which our spirit is a particular manifestation or image, so that through our inner experience we can obtain real knowledge of metaphysical substance. But if this supposition expresses the sole[116] condition of the possibility of metaphysics, it is clear that, in order for metaphysics to become real knowledge, it is necessary to *prove* the reality of the proposed identity of metaphysical substance and the knower, to prove that this substance really has a spiritual nature. Since there is no doubt that, in the real world of our experience, metaphysical substance is not given to us immediately, we can discover its nature only through its manifestation or action; and we can prove its spiritual nature only by demonstrating the spirituality of its manifestations in the real world. Since the distinctive feature of spiritual manifestation or action is purposefulness, i.e., action out of oneself presupposing *will* determined by *idea* as the goal, it follows that, to prove the spiritual nature of metaphysical substance, it is necessary to demonstrate that, in the world of our experience, besides those purposeful or rational actions which belong to separate particular subjects, there are also other purposeful or rational actions, which can thus belong only to the general metaphysical substance. Hartmann gives such an irrefutable proof in the fundamental part of his philosophy through the application of the true philosophical method, i.e., through the derivation from indisputable empirical data of that which is necessarily logically contained in them. In all spheres of our experience, in both external nature and the human world, Hartmann shows that, apart from the conscious activity of certain individuals, phenomena are determined by the purposeful action of the spiritual principle, which is independent of any particular consciousness and which, in its inner power, infinitely surpasses any particular consciousness, and is therefore called the *unconscious* (*das Unbewusste*) or the *superconscious* (*das Ueberbewusste*)[117] by Hartmann. Further, analyzing the logically generally recognized substratum of natural phenomena, i.e., matter, Hartmann showed that it is wholly reducible to the action of the spiritual elements of will and representation, attributes of that very same superconscious spiritual principle, so that materiality in the ordinary sense is only a *phenomenon*, an external relation to another, a result of the particular individuation of spiritual principles. Thus, the spiritual first principle conditions the whole material world with all of its forms and, therefore, is, in itself, free of these forms. It is free of space and of time. The principles of immediate existence and logical essence—will and idea—are inseparably united in it. It is an absolutely individual being, but one that is also universal. It is the all-one spirit: "The all-encompassing individual, which is all, the absolute individual, or the all-surpassing individual."[118]

Although we cannot immediately know the absolute being, nevertheless, by the means indicated we do come to know the following with perfect certainty: (1) *There is an all-one first principle of all that exists.* (2) *This all-one first principle has an indisputably spiritual character in its manifested reality, which we know in the domain of our experience.* (3) *This spiritual reality belongs to the first principle independently of our consciousness and is prior to it,* for that world in which we, with our consciousness, constitute only one of the phenomena (even if we serve as the goal of all the other phenomena) already presupposes in its determinate being the spiritual activity of the first principle (which refutes vulgar pantheism).

If we compare this view, logically derived from positive data, with Hartmann's still-born fantasies in which we find he expounds his principles *in abstracto* (particularly in the chapter "*Die letzten Principien*"), an indubitable contradiction will be revealed. In the first place, instead of the *absolutely concrete* and therefore *real* first principle, we find a grotesque duality of abstract hypostases—of will and idea. Further, in contrast to the logically necessary assertions of Hartmann himself that the metaphysical first principle is not subordinate to time and therefore cannot undergo any translational motion and development, here we learn that metaphysical will together with idea passed, at some specific moment, from a state of pure potentiality or nonbeing to actuality. We learn that metaphysical will accomplishes in time the cosmic process, and that, also in time, at some specific moment of the historical future, it will reverse its movement, going now from being to nonbeing. And then it may perhaps once again begin the same evolution. I have already sufficiently shown the absurdity of all this and explained its general cause. Its most immediate cause consists in an insufficiently clear understanding of the true philosophical method, as a result of which, alongside the application of this method in the scientific investigation of metaphysical principles in their actuality, there is also in Hartmann an abstract dialectic of these principles as something independent in itself. Here he necessarily falls victim to the general limitation of Western thought, isolating abstract concepts and raising them to the level of independent hypostases. This essential deficiency is even more characteristic of Schopenhauer's philosophy, in which the principle of that which exists immediately—will—and the principle of logical determination are not only thought abstractly, but also without any mutual correspondence, so that the significance of that which properly exists is ascribed only to will, which, however, is devoid of all content, while the ideal or logical principle is recognized as being only a subjective representation or merely a phantom.[119] In Hartmann the two principles are recognized as having equal rights, but since they are nevertheless conceived (in the transcendent part of his system) abstractly in themselves, their unification is only outward, merely an external juxtaposition.

Thus, although Schopenhauer and Hartmann are equally conscious of the one-sidedness of the two main tendencies of Western philosophy, equally avoid the opposite extremes of empty rationalism and meaningless empiricism, and even apply, to a greater or lesser degree, the true philosophical method in their metaphysical investigations (this refers especially to Hartmann), nevertheless an insufficiently clear understanding of the essence of this method does not permit them to effect an integral inner synthesis of the opposite principles. Their metaphysics therefore falls into frequent contradictions and utter absurdities. But if this deficiency in methodology, in the theory of knowledge, has an adverse influence on metaphysics, this also leads to deficiencies in *ethics,* or *practical philosophy.* For this part of philosophy has the same sort of necessary inner relation to the first two parts as these two parts have to each other. This relation is clearly revealed in the two indicated tendencies of Western philosophy. Just as both of these tendencies in their final development deny metaphysics, so they also deny practical philosophy as the doctrine of *that which should be.* Indeed, if all is reducible to present reality, to the determinate reality of our being, be it the reality of logical thought or that of sensuous consciousness, there is equally no place for that which should be; for this concept of that which should be contains the negation of present reality ("This should be" means that "This is not given by present reality") and therefore the assumption of something beyond its bounds. Indeed, as we found in the previous section, the consistent rationalism that we see in Hegel directly negates the very principles of practical or moral philosophy. And as regards extreme empiricism, even though some of its representatives (e.g., Mill) connect it with some simulacrum of ethics, the so-called *utilitarianism,* this is only a pitiful inconsistency. Carried to its logical end, the principle of utilitarianism is obviously equivalent to the complete negation of ethics. This is clear from the fact that, since empirical benefit is not something determinate in itself (for, depending on the circumstances, different things are beneficial to different people), and since nobody can determine the empirical benefit of another person (that would be arbitrariness and intolerable despotism), the sole practical norm becomes *what each person likes,* i.e., the immediate urges of individual nature. All possibility of any goal-setting and normative doctrine whatever therefore vanishes.

Both of the tendencies of Western philosophy that culminate in a complete denial of metaphysics first produce (in the unconscious and half-conscious stages of their development) corresponding metaphysical systems, and we find the same thing with respect to ethics. Of greatest interest in both tendencies are the moral doctrines that correspond to the middle or transitional moment in the development of these tendencies—a moment represented by Kant's critical philosophy in one of the tendencies and by the Anglo-Scottish school in the other. Kant founded the doctrine of moral *formalism*, in opposition to material ethics, which we find, for example, in ancient philosophy. The task of material ethics consists in determining the *supreme good* (*summum bonum*), which becomes the *ultimate goal* and *norm* of human activity. For Kant the question of good *in itself* did not have any meaning, since, according to the fundamental principle of his philosophy, we cannot know anything in itself. And since, on the other hand, no particular empirical good can serve a universal and ultimate goal, Kant could merely give a formal principle of morality, expressed in the form of the categorical imperative: "Always act in such a way that the rule of your actions could become a universal law," namely, in such a way that "in all of your actions humankind in the person of each of its representatives should be a goal, not a means, for you." But in order that we have something in this rule, it is necessary to define the meaning of the concept *goal* here: What does it mean to have humankind as a goal? The only possible answer (although one that obviously says nothing) would be as follows: To have humankind as a goal is always to have the *good* of humankind in mind. But it is clear that this principle would thereby get a material meaning prohibited by Kant, which, in fact, exposes the complete emptiness of formalistic morality. This morality has to subsist here on common phrases concerning human dignity, the absolute significance of the person, and so forth.

The corresponding moral doctrine in the empirical tendency, namely in the philosophy of *immediate feeling,* or *common sense,* founded by Reid, has a more positive meaning. Although this school is sometimes opposed to that of Locke, they essentially differ little. For even if this Scottish school recognizes certain primordial absolute principles, it recognizes them only as *empirical data*, as *facts of immediate experience*. Thus, for example, finding in our immediate consciousness the ineradicable absolute assurance that the external world exists, the Scottish school asserts this existence as an absolute and primordial truth. Likewise, finding in immediate consciousness the distinction between good and evil or between the moral and the immoral, this view affirms the moral principle as given empirically, on the basis of immediate feeling.[120] Further development defines the content of the moral principle; specifically, this principle is reduced to so-called sympathetic feelings. *Sympathy* for others is an immediate, primary *fact* of our spiritual nature and all morality is based on it. Truly, this fact is certain,[121] but just as certain and much more powerful is the opposite fact of *egoism*—the basis of immorality. It is true that the Scottish school asserts not only that the feeling of sympathy is a factual principle in our nature, but also that the immediate consciousness of the inner superiority of this moral principle over the opposite principle of egoism—a consciousness that constitutes what is called *conscience*—is also an immediate fact of our spiritual nature. In agreeing with this, one must remark, however, that to this *fact* of conscience in some people is opposed the fact that some people lack any conscience. One immediate feeling, one instinct, is not better or worse than another. The question is asked: Why should conscientious sympathy be preferred to unconscionable egoism? But only one answer is possible from the empirical point of view: Because the first is, in general (i.e., for all people in their totality), *more useful* than the second. But the morality of immediate feeling is thereby transformed into its opposite—into the morality of calculating utilitarianism.[122] The absoluteness of the moral sense is destroyed here in the relativity of external determinations, just as the absoluteness of the categorical imperative was destroyed by the omnipotence of the theoretical concept in Hegel's philosophy.

With the restoration of metaphysics—in Schopenhauer—ethics is also restored. The immediate sense of sympathy is recognized here, too, as the natural foundation of morality. But, in the first place, this sense is here defined philosophically as the identification of one's being with the being of others. Secondly, thanks to Schopenhauer's metaphysics, it gets from him a higher sanction, which it lacks in the Scottish school. In other words, since, according to Schopenhauer's metaphysical view, that which is in itself is one and identical in all individuals, and precisely this identity is affirmed immediately in the moral sense of sympathy, it follows that the moral sense is an expression of the true nature of that which is, whereas the opposite principle of egoism, which is the exclusive assertion of the isolated selfhood of particular entities, expresses not true being but that which is merely represented, being that is conditioned by the deceitful phantom of external reality. Thus, the very nature of the moral sense explains its absolute truthfulness in opposition to the exclusive self-assertion of egoism, and ethics is therefore based on metaphysics. On the other hand, the principle of this metaphysics is confirmed by the indisputable fact of the inner identification of different entities in the moral sense of sympathy, which can be explained only on the basis of this metaphysical principle.

But this defines and explains only the essential character of moral actions. There still remains the question of the *ultimate goal* of all activity or of the *supreme good*. This question is resolved by Schopenhauer, also on the basis of his metaphysical view. According to this view, the universal essence is expressed in empty and never-satisfied will and desire, so that being, in its essence, is *suffering*. The supreme (and unique) good, then, is nonbeing, and the ultimate goal is therefore determined to be

the *annihilation of being through the self-negation of the vital will*.
However, as a result of the indicated imperfection of his metaphysics, Schopenhauer, contradicting himself, admits the possibility of self-negation and self-annihilation for an individual
person, whose reality he recognizes to be illusory, so that he
derives even the first, imperfect level of morality from the
essence common to all individuals.

Hartmann is clearly conscious of this contradiction, and
therefore recognizes that the ultimate goal is attainable only for
the totality of that which exists by means of the *cosmic process*, as
the final result of this process. The truth contained in Hartmann's practical philosophy consists, first of all, in the recognition that *the supreme good, the ultimate goal of life, is not contained
within the limits of the given actuality, in the world of finite reality*,
but on the contrary, *is attained only through the annihilation of this
world*. Secondly, it consists in the recognition that this ultimate
goal is attainable not for a separate individual in his separateness, but only for the whole world of entities, so that this attainment *is necessarily conditioned by the course of universal cosmic
development*. The truth contained in both of these propositions
flows directly from the demonstrated truth of the fundamental
metaphysical principle according to which the *all-one spirit* is
affirmed as the truly existent, absolute first principle and end of
everything that exists. It is indeed clear that, in the case of this
principle, the existence in which the direct opposite of that
which truly exists is given (the discordant individuality of separate entities, which is based on external, material determinateness, in which that which truly exists is manifested as something
other, alien, and unknown, revealed only by the greatest efforts
of speculation), the existence in which true reality belongs to
particular relative phenomena, whereas that which truly exists,
the integral spirit, is taken as an empty phantom, or as a dead
substance, an existence based on the deceit of representation

(and such precisely is our actual existence and the whole of our real world)—this existence must, of course, be recognized as untrue, as something that *should not be*. And the true goal is to remove the exclusiveness of this existence, thus restoring a true relation between the universal, absolute principle and its particular manifestations. It is also clear that, once the integral, concrete spirit, positing all reality, is recognized as the absolute principle, one must recognize that everything that happens—the cosmic process—is a manifestation of that very same spirit. Therefore, the end of this process—the annihilation of the existing world in its *exclusive* reality—is necessarily posited by that same all-one spirit. Consequently, for this reason alone, the attainment of the ultimate goal cannot have that subjective significance which is given to it by Schopenhauer.

On the other hand, it is clear that when Hartmann, having demonstrated in a fully founded manner the negative character of the cosmic process and its ultimate result or goal, asserts that in this ultimate result not only is the present reality of the finite real world in its exclusive self-assertion removed (as is certainly true), but this removal is a complete *annihilation*, a transition to pure nonbeing—it is clear that such an assertion not only is absurd in itself (as we showed previously) but also directly contradicts Hartmann's fundamental metaphysical principle. Indeed, the end of the cosmic process, in the first place, cannot be the absolute annihilation of *all that exists* because the absolute all-one spirit, which is completely *independent of time* (as Hartmann himself admits), cannot in itself be determined by the *temporal* cosmic process. Therefore, this spirit unchangeably remains in its absolute being *before*, *during*, and *after* the cosmic process. This process and its ultimate result, therefore, have significance only for phenomenal being, for the world of real phenomena. But, in the second place, for this world too the end of the process is not annihilation in the absolute sense—because what is recognized as the absolute principle is not an abstract substance, not an *empty unity*, but the concrete, all-one, *all-embracing spirit*. And this spirit does not have a negative relation to the other, to particular being, but, on the contrary, itself posits this being. Therefore, at the end of the cosmic process the removal of present actuality is an annihilation not of particular being itself but only of its *exclusive self-assertion*, its external peculiarity and separateness. This is an annihilation not of the world of phenomena in general, but only of material, mechanical phenomena, of the monstrous phantom of the dead external reality of material separateness—a phantom that, in the theoretical sphere, has already disappeared before the light of philosophical idealism, and that in the sphere of practical actuality will disappear in the culmination of the cosmic process. Therefore, the ultimate end of all is not Nirvana but "the restitution of all things"[123]—the kingdom of spirits, as the complete manifestation of the all-one.

Thus, after those obvious absurdities in the "philosophy of the unconscious" which follow from its relative limitedness and are found to contradict the fundamental principles are removed, we get the following general results, which, at the same time, are also the results of the whole of the Western philosophical development, because, as we have seen, Hartmann's philosophy is the legitimate and necessary product of this development:

(1) In *logic* or the theory of knowledge: *Recognition of the one-sidedness and therefore falsity of both tendencies of philosophical knowledge* in the West, namely the *purely rationalistic* tendency, which gives only *possible* knowledge, and the *purely empirical* tendency, which *does not give any* knowledge—and thus the *affirmation of the true philosophical method.*

(2) In *metaphysics*: *Recognition of the concrete all-one spirit as the absolute total principle*, instead of the former abstract substances and hypostases.

(3) In *ethics*: Recognition that *the ultimate goal and supreme good are attained only by the totality of entities by means of the necessary and absolutely purposeful course of cosmic development, the end of which is the annihilation of the exclusive self-assertion of particular entities in their material dissension and their restoration as the kingdom of spirits, embraced by the universality of the absolute spirit.*

Here it turns out that these ultimate necessary results of the *Western* philosophical development affirm, in the form of *rational knowledge*, the *same* truths that have been affirmed in the form of *faith* and *spiritual contemplation* by the great theological teachers of the *East* (in part the ancient East and especially the Christian East). Based, on the one hand, on the data of *positive science*, this *philosophy*, on the other hand, extends its hand to *religion*. The realization of this *universal synthesis* of science, philosophy, and religion—the first and far from perfect principles of which we have in the "philosophy of the superconscious"—must be the supreme goal and ultimate result of intellectual development. The attainment of this goal will be the restoration of the complete inner *unity of the intellectual world* in the fulfillment of the testament of ancient wisdom: "The whole and the unwhole, the convergent and the divergent, harmony and discord are linked; one from all and all from one [are formed]."[124]

Appendix

※

AUGUSTE COMTE'S
THEORY OF THE THREE PHASES IN
THE INTELLECTUAL DEVELOPMENT OF
HUMANKIND

At the end of the foregoing inquiry, I showed that the universal synthesis of theology, philosophical metaphysics, and positive science is the necessary culmination of the philosophical development, a logical and historical necessity. By contrast, the well-known theory of Auguste Comte defines theology, metaphysics, and positive science as three *successive* phases in the intellectual development of humankind. In this theory the concluding stage of this development is positive science alone, whereas theology and metaphysics are recognized as only preliminary, transitional stages. It is clear that this implicitly negates the possibility of the synthesis affirmed by me. I must therefore examine this supposed law, especially since, as we have seen, it constitutes the main, if not the sole, basis of Comte's whole system of positivism, which stands or falls with it.

French positivism's pretension to universality is greater than that of any other system. Its representatives were convinced that positivism must become the universal world-view for the entire civilized world, must become that which papism was in the Middle Ages.

As Comte states:

> Positive philosophy can serve as the unique solid foundation for social reorganization, which must end that state of crisis in which the most civilized nations have found themselves for such a long time. . . . I do not have to prove that the world is guided and moved by *ideas*, or, in other words, that the whole social mechanism [sic] is ultimately based on opinions [sic]. In particular, the great political and moral crisis of contemporary societies is caused, in the final analysis, by intellectual anarchy. Indeed, our greatest evil consists in the profound disharmony existing at the present time among all minds in relation to all the basic principles, the stability and determinateness of which are the first condition of a true social order. Until individual minds unanimously accept a certain number [sic] of common ideas capable of forming a common social doctrine, until then nations, despite all possible political palliatives, will necessarily remain in a revolutionary state, actually admitting only temporary institutions. It is just as certain that, once a union of minds in a communion of principles is achieved, all the needed institutions will necessarily proceed from this union without any significant convulsions, since the greatest disorder will be dissipated by this fact alone.[1]

To produce such "a union of minds in a communion of principles" and thereby to provide a "firm foundation for social reorganization and a truly normal order of things" is precisely

what constitutes the purpose of positivism or positive philosophy, according to its founder. But to understand the true nature
and character of positive philosophy, says Comte, one must first
cast one's glance at the common intellectual development of
humankind, the result of which development is positivism. This
development is determined by a fundamental historical law,
which constitutes Comte's greatest discovery, both according to
him and according to his followers:

> This law consists in the fact that each of our main con-
> cepts, each branch of our knowledge, passes successively
> through three different theoretical states: the *theological* or
> fictive state (*état fictif*); the *metaphysical* or abstract state;
> and the *scientific* or positive state. In other words, by its
> nature the human mind successively employs—in each of
> its inquiries—three methods, essentially different in char-
> acter and even radically opposed to one another: first, the
> theological method, then the metaphysical method, and
> finally the positive method. From this we get three kinds
> of mutually exclusive philosophies or general systems
> embracing phenomena as a whole: the first system is the
> necessary point of departure of the human mind; the third
> system is its fixed and definitive state; the second serves
> only as a transition.[2]

What the first two systems are—we shall see later. We shall
now examine the nature of the final and definitive state of the
human mind, i.e., positivism. Comte says:

> In the positive state, the human mind, recognizing the
> impossibility of absolute knowledge, ceases to seek the
> principles and purposes of the world. It refuses to inquire
> into the inner causes of phenomena and occupies itself
> exclusively with the discovery of their effective laws, i.e.,
> with their invariable relations of succession and similarity,
> uniting here observation with reasoning. The explanation
> of the facts, reduced to its real terms, is nothing but the
> establishment of a connection between distinct separate

phenomena and certain general facts, the number of which is gradually decreasing with the development of science. The perfection of the positive system, toward which this system is constantly tending (but which it will, most probably, never reach), would consist in the possibility of representing all distinct observable phenomena as particular cases of one general fact, for example, gravitation.[3]

The fundamental character of positive philosophy consists in the fact that it considers all phenomena as subordinate to immutable natural *laws*, the precise discovery of which and the reduction of which to the smallest possible number constitutes the goal of all our efforts. The search for so-called *causes*, whether primary or final (*causes finales*, i.e., goals), is recognized by positive philosophy as completely inaccessible for us and meaningless. It is useless to insist on this principle, which is acknowledged by all people who have occupied themselves with the empirical sciences. Everyone knows in fact that, even in our most perfect positive explanations, we are not claiming to expound causes that produce phenomena, because then we would only be putting off the question. We are only accurately analyzing the conditions of phenomena and linking them to one another by means of normal relations of succession and similarity.[4]

The positive method described in this way as the general and unique method for all scientific knowledge unites all sciences and thereby produces from them a single system of knowledge, which Comte calls positive philosophy. Thus, here are those great principles which must create the new world! The union of the so-called positive or natural[5] sciences by means of one general method, which confines these sciences to the knowledge of observed phenomena and their external relationships or laws— that is what positivism consists in. For the time being, let us leave aside the question of whether natural science can, by its nature, form a universal world-view. The positivists consider this possible. Let us try to take their point of view.

What is necessary for the natural sciences united by positivism to really form a single universal world-view? This will evidently be possible only if the unification of the *sciences* is, at the same time, the total unification of the whole of human consciousness. But for this it is necessary to prove that the actual content of consciousness coincides with the content of positive science, i.e., is confined to external phenomena and their relationships, whereas everything else found in consciousness does not have and cannot have any reality, since it is only an invented conceit or a barren abstraction. Since any content of our consciousness that transcends the bounds of relative phenomena has the character either of religion or of philosophical metaphysics, positivism should not base itself on the factual inconsistency of one form of religious and philosophical opinion or another. It should base itself only on the general insufficiency of religion and metaphysical philosophy as such.

Precisely such a general insufficiency of religion and metaphysical philosophy is asserted by Comte in his historical law, according to which, as we have seen, these two views, under the names *état théologique* and *état métaphysique*,[6] have a necessarily temporary, preliminary character, as preparatory stages in the development of humankind. Having become conscious of their insufficiency (according to the ineffectiveness or unattainability of their object), humankind passes to the scientific or positive world-view as the sole certain and conclusive one. If this law is correct, positivism does, in fact, receive a solid foundation and also the sole foundation that it can receive by its very nature. Indeed, as we have seen, the fundamental principle of positivism consists in the denial of any absolute or inner principle, in the exclusive recognition of external phenomena or facts as relative.[7] It is clear that this principle can be proved only negatively, i.e., by proving the inconsistency of the opposite principle, of all that has been recognized and is recognized as absolute. Furthermore, this proof must have a factual character, since for positivism only fact has meaning. But on the other hand, in accordance with positivism's essential claim to universality, this fact too must be universal. It is precisely such a universal fact, proving the inconsistency of every absolute view, that is expressed in the law of three phases. But the question is asked: Is this law correct?

This question can be separated into two questions: (1) How correctly do positivists understand the religious and philosophical (metaphysical) view? That is to say, to what extent does that which they describe under the names *état théologique* and *état métaphysique* correspond to the proper content of actual religion and actual metaphysical philosophy? (2) Have religion, metaphysical philosophy, and positive science had in actual history that relation of *succession* which is asserted in the law of three phases?

Comte defines the essence of religion as follows:

> In the theological state, the human mind, directing its inquiries chiefly at the intimate nature of beings, at the first and last causes that strike it, in a word, at absolute knowledge, represents phenomena as produced by the direct and continuous action of more or less numerous supernatural agents, whose arbitrary intervention explains all the apparent anomalies of the universe.[8]

Further, according to Comte, with the development of the theological system the initial multiplicity of independent agents is replaced by a single being, to whose will all phenomena are attributed. For Comte religion thus appears and exists solely to *explain* external phenomena as their initial *theory*, an unsatisfactory and arbitrary theory, which humankind therefore rejects in proportion to its progressive development, replacing it with other theories, first with metaphysical ones, and finally with scientific or positive ones. Here are the words of Comte himself:

> If, on the one hand, every positive theory must be based
> on observations, it is just as clear, on the other hand, that
> for correct observation the human mind needs some theo-
> ry. Thus, compelled, on the one hand, by the necessity of
> observing in order to form actual theories, and, on the
> other hand, by the equally imperious necessity of produc-
> ing for itself some sort of theories, in order to carry out
> successive observations, the human mind would at the
> very beginning have found itself confined in a vicious
> circle if, fortunately, it had not discovered a natural way
> out for itself through the spontaneous development of the-
> ological conceptions, which have given a solid foundation
> for its efforts and food for its activity. . . .[9]

The development of the religious world-view is described
by Comte in the following way: Phenomena are first explained
by likening them to human actions, since life and independent
activity are attributed to all the objects of the external world.
This is *fetishism*. Then, "a stronger hypothesis," to use Comte's
expression, appears in the form of *polytheism*. This "hypothesis"
explains every phenomenon as the action of a particular supernatural being, and for every phenomenon a new supernatural
agent is invented. Finally, when people begin to remark in phenomena their regularity, the constancy of their relations, polytheism is replaced by *monotheism*. That is, all phenomena are
attributed to the action of one transcendent being.

Such an explanation of religion is undoubtedly distinguished by simplicity and clarity. Its only deficiency is that it
bears very little relation to true religion. In the first place, when
it is asserted that religion *came into being* as a theory or hypothesis to explain phenomena, this involves the absurd assumption
that, in that primordial era in which religious conceptions must
be considered to have originated, human beings were abstract
theoreticians to the same degree that contemporary scientists
are now. Contemporary scientists really do require various

theories and hypotheses to explain natural phenomena, because for them these phenomena appear to be something external and alien. But for ancient human beings, as language and mythology prove with certainty, natural phenomena in our sense did not exist at all, and there was therefore nothing to explain. For ancient human beings, all that existed was revealed directly, as an expression and action of an animate being or animate beings. Ancient human beings not only spoke mythologically but even thought mythologically (according to Steinthal's just comment). Therefore, what Comte calls fetishism and polytheism, i.e., mythology, is a certain direct mode of seeing. To consider it, as Comte does, an invented theory is just as absurd as to see an invented theory in that spiritualization of material objects which is remarked in the majority of children even in our own time. Science long ago rejected those explanations according to which the general and essential phenomena of human life were considered products of conscious deliberation or premeditated design. The theory that society and the state have their origin in a contract was rejected long ago as has been the theory that language has its origin in an arbitrary condition. Just as inconceivable, given the current state of science, is Comte's explanation of religion as an invented hypothesis.

If Comte's view of religion is beneath all criticism even with reference to the elementary, mythological forms of religion, the groundlessness of this view becomes completely obvious with reference to the more perfect religions. As we remarked above, if Comte's law is to have the kind of universal significance that positivists attribute to it, it must refer in its terms *theology* and *metaphysics* to religion *in general* and to speculative philosophy[10] *in general*, i.e., to *all* possible religions and to *all* possible speculations. But even if we retreat from this requirement as too rigorous, we certainly have the right to demand that at least all the actually existing religious and metaphysical views conform to the theological and metaphysical phases that Comte has defined. For, otherwise, what significance could be possessed by a scientific law to which the actual phenomena that enter into its domain do not conform? However, leaving metaphysics aside for the moment, we find not only that certain religions completely fail to conform to Comte's "theological state," but these religions are even the most important and perfect ones. For instance, what relation to Comte's conception of religion can Brahmanism have, since it considers the whole world of phenomena to be a deceitful phantom, a product of ignorance, and its supreme goal is the liberation of man from this phantom of phenomena, in union with the absolute being of Brahma? Or in what manner can such a religion as Buddhism occupy itself with the "explanation of phenomena" (for Comte posits that the essence of religion consists in this), since the fundamental dogma of Buddhism is the complete nothingness, the "emptiness" of all that exists, and its supreme goal is Nirvana, the complete extinction of all life? And what about Christianity? Whether one posits its essence in its dogmatics or in its moral doctrine, in neither case does it conform to Comte's conception of religion. Indeed, what connection to the "explanation of observable phenomena (*explication des phénomènes observables*)" can the main Christian dogmas of the Trinity, the Incarnation, and the Resurrection have, on the one hand, and what connection can Christian morality have to it, on the other? However these three religions may differ, all of them have this in common, that, in their principle, they have a *negative* relation to the present reality and see as their essential task the *liberation* of humanity from the evil and suffering that are necessary in the existing world. They are all religions of salvation. Thus, neither the theoretical principle nor the practical task of these widespread religions has any relation to what positivism posits as the essence of religion. None of this poses any difficulty for Comte, for he is simply in ignorance of the content of the actual religions. In his lengthy exposition of intellectual development he does not say a word about the most important doctrines of the East, and his arguments concerning Christianity contain a series of astonishing curiosities, of which, for the sake of illustration, I will mention only two: Comte asserts that Christ was *only* a political adventurer and, on the basis of the fact that Protestantism has a negative attitude toward the externalities of cult, Comte assures us that it is only a reproduction of . . . Mohammedanism.

Given a positive view of religion as a certain explanation of phenomena, it is necessary to assert that paganism was supplanted by Christianity because the latter gives a better explanation of natural phenomena. Indeed, the positivist Mill is not very far from such an assertion. In his opinion, monotheism is in greater accord with the positivist type of thought, and the transition from polytheism to monotheism, i.e., more precisely, to Christianity, was chiefly conditioned by the development of positive knowledge, since toward the time of the appearance of Christianity

> . . . the belief in the immutable laws of nature as constituting the basis of the positivist type of thought was slowly making its way in proportion to the progress made by observation and experiment in, step by step, discovering in classes of phenomena those laws to which they are actually subordinate.

Mill then asks himself:

> Thus by what means were the leading minds of Rome prepared for monotheism? By the development of a practical sense of the immutability of the laws of nature. Monotheism was naturally progressing toward this belief, whereas polytheism was necessarily in disharmony with it. Thus, the transition of the theological system from polytheism to monotheism was accomplished under the direct influence of positive knowledge.[11]

In order to be consistent, Mill should have asserted that the semibarbaric tribes of Arabia and Mauritania that adopted

Mohammed's monotheism were prepared for this by the development among them of positive knowledge. There appears to be no need to linger at greater length over such absurdities. It is too obvious that in their explanation of the theological state the positivists do not even touch upon the content of real religion.

The second phase of the development of humankind according to Comte is the "metaphysical state," representing the transition from the theological to the positive state, which is to replace it. The essence of this transitional view is defined by Comte as follows:

> In the metaphysical state, which, basically, is only a general modification of the theological one, supernatural agents are replaced by abstract forces, by real entities (*véritables entités*) or personified abstractions, which are inherent in various beings of the world and are understood as capable of producing, by themselves, all observable phenomena, the explanation of which consists in the fact that a corresponding entity is assigned to each phenomenon.

Such a conception of speculative philosophy does not belong to Comte alone, but, as we shall see below, has its basis in the very nature of positivism and is therefore accepted and developed by all positivists. Mill, for instance, asserts that the metaphysical world-view consists in the fact that, in every phenomenon or object, "something" is presupposed that produces this phenomenon or acts in this object. "When the need was felt," he says, "to designate this something by a determinate word, one began to call it the nature of objects, their essence, the capabilities dwelling in them, and by many other names." If Mill had wanted to present a classic specimen of such metaphysics, he would have found it, of course, not in philosophical systems but in Moliere's comedy *Le Malade imaginaire*, in the famous explanation, "Opium puts people to sleep, because it has a sleep-inducing power."[12] But the positivists are convinced that such a manner of thought constitutes a general phase in the intellectual development of the whole of humankind, a phase that succeeds the religious world-view. First, in Mill's opinion, these metaphysical conceptions served only as intermediaries between the theological conception, Divinity, and real objects. "However, in consequence of the habit of attributing to abstract substances not only substantial existence but also real active activity [sic], the entities remained alone in their place when faith in Divinity began to decline and disappear."

If other arguments of the positivists concerning metaphysics were more solid and were, moreover, expounded in a form less absurd and vulgar, we could accept them as a fair indication of that formal deficiency of Western philosophy which was explained in the third chapter of the present inquiry, a deficiency which consists in the constant isolation and hypostasization of general logical concepts. But even in this case it would be an unforgivable misunderstanding on the part of the positivists to confuse this formal deficiency of Western philosophy with the very task and essence of speculative thought. Whatever the case might be, to anyone at all familiar with the history of philosophy, all the arguments of the positivists concerning metaphysics can only appear ridiculous, and there is no need for me to refute them after I have, in the present book, expounded the essential content of existing philosophical systems. The possibility of positive concepts of metaphysics is explained only by complete ignorance of true philosophy, an ignorance which, with reference to Comte, is confirmed by his disciple and biographer Littré.

Thus, the first of the questions posed by me receives a negative answer: What the positivists describe under the names "theological and metaphysical states" does not in any way correspond to the proper content of actual religion and actual philosophical metaphysics. As regards the second question, concerning the historical relationship of religion, philosophy, and positive science, it is first necessary to remark that the positivists already make a crude blunder by placing in a single sequential series religious, speculative, and scientific views as general phases in the intellectual development of *all* of humankind, whereas, in the first place, religion and philosophy are, in fact, mutually incommensurate in the sense that philosophy, being a work of personal reason, has always formed the views only of individual persons, an insignificant minority. By contrast, the world-views of social units, whole nations and tribes, have always had only a religious character. Secondly, religion and philosophy (metaphysics) on the one hand and positive science on the other are mutually incommensurate with respect to their object, for science deals only with phenomena, with the world of appearance, whereas religion and metaphysical philosophy, pushing aside the appearance of external forms and relations, poses as its task the theoretical and practical knowledge of that which truly is and not only appears. From this it is clear that, among religion, metaphysics, and positive science, there cannot be any relationship of succession, any substitution, for such a relationship is possible only between homogeneous objects. And, in fact, from the very beginning of the intellectual development of humanity we find religious faith, philosophical speculations, and positive observations existing simultaneously in their distinct spheres. Thus, for example, in ancient India, alongside national beliefs, there always existed among the intellectual minority a developed philosophy and the rudiments of a true science. We find the same thing among the Assyrians and Egyptians, not to mention the Greeks.

Thus, "theology," "metaphysics," and "positive science," with the meaning given to them by the positivists, have never actually existed in the sense of successive general world-views or sequential general phases in the inner development of all humankind. Therefore, Comte's law, based on these concepts, does not have any reality in the sense of a universal historical law. But it would be very unlikely if this law were a pure fiction, based on nothing; indeed, we have no need to assert that. The definitions and explanations of the positivists themselves clearly show what the true particular significance of their pseudouniversal law consists in, what corresponds to this law in the actual historical development of the human mind.

The sole object of investigation of the positive or natural sciences consists, without doubt, in observable phenomena, of both external nature and humankind, insofar as the latter is manifested externally. But since these phenomena by their very nature, as empirical phenomena, constitute an infinite, indeterminate multiplicity and diversity, their truly scientific investigation, i.e., the study of their general relationships or laws, could only arise at a later stage of intellectual development, when the preceding experience had given sufficient material for positive science and the formal improvement of theoretical capabilities had made it possible to precisely define the domain of scientific investigation and to work out a general and true scientific method. Therefore, although the rudiments of positive science and therefore of the scientific method had already existed in the most ancient times alongside religious beliefs and philosophical speculations, these rudiments were limited to an insignificant portion of the scientific domain. Meanwhile, the remaining phenomena, more complex, were considered not from the point of view of their law-conforming relationships but were explained *directly* on the basis of other, ready-made views, views which, primordially, were precisely religious views. This direct explanation of the greater part of natural phenomena on the basis of religious conceptions constitutes the whole of what, in the actual history of the mind, corresponds to the "theological state" of the positivists. Here it is clear, first of all, that if phenomena were explained on the basis of religious representations, this already presupposed the existence of these religious conceptions in the minds of primitive human beings prior to any relation to phenomena, the existence in these minds of religious conceptions as something more indisputable for them than the phenomena themselves. For one can explain something only by means of what is clearer and more certain that what is being explained. Therefore, it is not possible to derive religion from a certain explanation of phenomena as the positivists do, for such an explanation already presupposes the existence of religious conceptions as an object of absolute faith. From this it is clear, in the second place, that "theology" in this sense is by no means religion itself, but only a certain application of religious conceptions to the immediate explanation of particular phenomena. And for anyone not completely devoid of the ability to think, the difference between the proper content of a certain view and an application of this view outside of its sphere is obvious. It is therefore obvious that when such an external application of a given view is rejected as illegitimate, this does not in any way refute the view itself. Therefore, if it is right to reject the immediate explanation of particular phenomena on the basis of religious conceptions, this has nothing to do with religion itself.

The same thing must be said about the second, or metaphysical, phase. Its true significance consists in the fact that when, with the development of knowledge, the direct explanation of particular phenomena on the basis of religious conceptions became impossible, but positive science had not yet evolved to a point where it could encompass the whole of its natural domain, it remained but to explain separate phenomena directly on the basis of the general concepts of philosophical metaphysics, i.e., on the basis of some metaphysical systems or other. And here it is also perfectly clear that, in the first place, such explanations already presuppose philosophical metaphysics and that, in the second place (as is already clear from the first proposition), these explanations constitute only a certain application of philosophical metaphysics outside of its own sphere, but by no means philosophical metaphysics itself. The latter therefore does not suffer any detriment from the fact that those metaphysical explanations of phenomena are rejected. If one, together with the positivists, is to call such a mode of explanation a metaphysical state, it must be noted that this was the state of only a few philosophers, but by no means the universal state of the human mind, and that it very soon ceded its place to the true scientific and positive method. According to the latter, natural phenomena as phenomena are studied only relatively, in their external causality or in their mutual relations of contiguity and similarity. Only the laws of phenomena are studied, i.e., some constant sequence or other which puts them in a determinate order with respect to one another. As is fitting, the world of externality is studied in an external manner.

Thus, Comte's historical law is perfectly correct if it is applied only to the study of external phenomena, but it is meaningless as the general law of the whole of intellectual development. Referring only to the study of external facts or observable phenomena and justly excluding from this study all secondary elements, both religious and philosophical, Comte's law obviously has nothing to do with religion and philosophical metaphysics, which, in themselves, have nothing to do with external phenomena and their study. Their domain and task are wholly other, and therefore to assert that positive science must replace and is already replacing the religious and metaphysical world-view is simply meaningless. "However far a plane is extended," says Schopenhauer, "it will never receive a cubic content; in the same way, whatever perfection natural science may attain, by its very nature it can never replace (religious and philosophical) metaphysics."

The positivists themselves involuntarily and probably unconsciously admit that the historical law of three phases has significance only for the development of the natural sciences, and that by theology and metaphysics one must properly understand only theological and metaphysical elements in the domain of natural science. Thus, for example, Comte, saying that the development of positive philosophy began with Bacon and Descartes, adds: "from this memorable epoch one can clearly discern the progress of theological and positive philosophy and the decline of metaphysical philosophy."[13] It is clear that metaphysical philosophy here can mean only metaphysical elements in the natural sciences, but by no means true philosophical metaphysics—for the latter has not only not gone into decline since the time of Descartes but, on the contrary, has since then only begun its true evolution, which has reached its highest peak only in the present century (I mean speculative philosophy). In another place Comte speaks of his historical law:

> It is sufficient but to express such a law for its correctness to be confirmed at once by all who have reliable knowledge about the general history of the sciences. In the past each of these sciences which now has truly attained the positive state consisted, in essence, of metaphysical abstractions. In its earliest stages, each was even exclusively guided by theological concepts.[14]

The following words of Mill even more clearly confirm our conclusion:

> Anyone who has had the possibility of tracing the history of the various natural sciences knows that the positive explanation of facts has gradually taken the place of the theological and metaphysical explanation, proportionally to the rate at which the progress of research has brought into the light of day an ever-increasing number of immutable laws for phenomena.

Thus, the positivists themselves must admit that the law of three phases refers only to the domain of the natural sciences. This law actually proves only that external relative phenomena as such must be studied in an external relative manner. It proves, in other words, that the positive sciences must be positive, that the natural sciences must be natural, something that nobody would dispute.

Despite all this, the positivists are certain that the law of three phases annuls religion and metaphysical philosophy. Such a misunderstanding is easy to understand. The basic principle, or essence, of positivism consists in the fact that, besides observable phenomena as external facts, nothing exists for us, and that the relative knowledge of these phenomena therefore constitutes the sole actual content of human consciousness. For positivism, everything else is completely alien and inaccessible. Given such a basic conviction, in such a state of consciousness, what must religion and philosophical metaphysics be for positivists? The inner, proper content of religions and philosophical metaphysics does not exist for positivists by the very nature of their world-view. This content is completely invisible to them; they see religion and philosophical metaphysics only where they stop being themselves and venture into what is for them the alien territory of particular external phenomena, the only territory accessible to positivists. Therefore, in religion, positivists must see only mythological explanations of external phenomena, and in metaphysics they must see only their abstract explanations. And here they triumphantly point to the fact, expressed in Comte's historical law, that such mythological and abstract explanations of phenomena are removed and disappear with the successes of scientific development, ceding their place to positive science. Positivists are confident that this fact proves the groundlessness of religion and philosophical metaphysics *in general* and thus leads to the desired result, i.e., to positivism as the exclusive world-view. But such a universal meaning can be ascribed to this law (which, as has been shown and as the positivists themselves must admit, proves only the groundlessness of the application of religious and metaphysical views to the study of particular phenomena as such) only if one confuses religion and metaphysical philosophy *per se* with a certain external and truly incorrect application of religious and metaphysical concepts. This confusion is based on the exclusive nature of positivism, which has no access to the proper content of religion and philosophical metaphysics. Therefore, if positivism rejects religion and metaphysical philosophy, this is solely because it *fails to understand* their content.[15]

In order to justify its claims and to bring its task to completion, positivism had to rise *above* other views—religious and philosophical—and thus to refute them. But in fact it turns out to be *beneath* them, since they are *incomprehensible* to it.

The fundamental principle of positivism as a *universal view* consists in the exclusive recognition of relative phenomena and therefore in the rejection of any absolute view, either religious or philosophical. The sole basis of this rejection that is possible for positivism, namely Comte's law of three phases, proves to be completely groundless in this sense, for in no wise does it touch upon the proper content of religion and metaphysical philosophy. It is clear that positivism's claim to be the universal world-view is completely unfounded. Apart from this claim, positivism is reducible to a certain system of particular empirical sciences without universal significance. Thus, if positivists affirm this system of empirical sciences as the only true knowledge and deny any absolute religious and philosophical principle, this affirmation and denial are only a natural consequence of the inherent *limitations* of positivism.

Notes

1.   However, according to the astonishing presuppositions of some spiri-
      tists, works of artistic genius are actually produced by spirits of the
      dead, who inspire the artist. So asserts, for example, Robert Dale Owen
      in his book *The Debatable Land between This World and the Next.*

2.   "Vera enim auctoritas rectae rationi non obsistit, neque recta ratio verae
      auctoritati. Ambo siquidem ex una fonte, divina videlicet sapientia, man-
      are, dubium non est." *Ioannis Scoti opera omnia* (Complete Works of John
      Scotus Erigena), ed. Floss, p. 511. [The original Latin, Greek, French, or
      German passages sprinkled throughout Solovyov's text have been
      replaced by the English translations, and the foreign-language texts have
      been moved to the Notes.—Trans.]

3.   "*Magister*: Non ignoras, ut opinor, majoris dignitatis esse quod est natu-
      ra, quam quod prius est tempore. *Discipulus*: Hoc paene omnibus
      notum est. *Magister*: Rationem priorem esse natura, auctoritatem vero
      tempore didicimus." Ibid., p. 513.

4.   "Quamvis enim natura simul cum tempore creata sit, non tamen ab ini-
      tio temporis atque naturae coepit esse auctoritatis. Ratio vero cum natu-
      ra ac tempore ex principio rerum orta est. *Discipulus*: Et hoc ipsa ratio
      edocet. Auctoritas ex vera ratione processit, ratio autem nequaquam ex
      auctoritate. Omnis enim auctoritas, quae vera ratione non approbatur,
      infirma videtur esse. Vera autem ratio, quoniam suis virtutibus rata
      atque immutabilis munitur, nullius auctoritatis adstipulatione roborari
      indiget. Nil enim aliud mihi videtur esse vera auctoritas, nisi rationis vir-
      tute reperta veritas, et a sanctis patribus ad posteritatis utilatatem literis
      commendata. Sed forte tibi aliter veidetur? *Magister*: Nullo modo.
      Ideoque prius ratione utendum est in his quae nunc instant ac deinde
      auctoritate."—Ibid.

5. Cf. Ueberweg, *Grundriss der Geschichte der Philosophie* (A History of Philosophy), part 2, p. 117.

6. *Petri Abaelardi opera omnia* (Complete Works of Peter Abelard), Migne, p. 1349.

7. A detailed exposition of these philosophical doctrines of the fifteenth and sixteenth centuries can be found in Stöckl, *Geschichte der Philosophie des Mittelalters* (History of Medieval Philosophy), 3 B.

8. "Toutes les choses que nous concevons clairement et distinctement, sont vraies de la façon dont nous les concevons." Therefore, "les choses, que l'on conçoit clairement et distinctement être des substances diverses, sont en effet des substances réellement distinctes les unes des autres."— Descartes, *Oeuvres* (Works), ed. Jules Simon, p. 62.

9. "De cela seul," Descartes says further, "que je puis tirer de ma pensée l'idée de quelque chose, il s'ensuit, que tout ce que je reconnais clairement et distinctement appartenir a cette chose, lui appartient en effet." Ibid., p. 107.

10. "Pour ce que d'un coté j'ai une claire et distincte idée de moi même en tant que je suis seulement une chose qui pense et non étendue, et que d'un autre j'ai une idée distincte du corps en tant qu'il est seulement une chose étendue et qui ne pense point, il est certain, que moi, c'est à dire mon âme, par laquelle je suis ce que je suis, est entièrement et véritablement distincte de mon corps."—Ibid., p. 117.

11. Descartes, *Principien der Philosophie* (Principles of Philosophy), translated by Kirchmann.

12. "les actes de la volonté, c'est à dire les jugements." Descartes, *Oeuvres*, p. 103.

13. "Per substantiam intelligo id, quod in se est et per se concipitur, hoc est id, cujus conceptus non indiget conceptu alterius rei, a quo formari debeat." Spinoza, *Ethica* (Ethics), part 1, def. 3.

14. "Per attributam intelligo id, quod intellectus de substantia percipit tamquam ejus essentiam constituens." Ibid., def. 4.

15. "Per modum intelligo affectiones sive id, quod in alio est, per quod etiam concipitur." Ibid., def. 5.

16. "Res particulares nihil sunt, nisi Dei attributorum affectiones sive modi, quibis Dei attributa certo et determinato modo exprimuntur." Ibid., prop. 25 corollary.

17. *Ethica*, book 1, prop. 17, schol.

18. "Ordo et connexio idearum idem est ac ordo et connexio rerum." Ibid., prop. 7.

19. *Ethica,* book 1, prop. 17, schol.

20. "Substantia, natura est prius suis affectionibus." *Ethica,* book 1, prop. 1.

21. "Depositis affectionibus et in se considerata." Ibid., prop. 5, demonst.

22. "Causa sui, cujus essentia involvit existentiam." Ibid., def. 1.

23. "Individua omnia quamvis diversis gradubus animata tamen sunt." *Ethica,* book 2, prop. 13, schol.

24. "Si l'essence du corps consistait dans l'étendue, cette étendue seule devrait suffire pour rendre raison de toutes les propriétés du corps. Mais cela n'est point. Nous remarquons dans la matière une qualité, par laquelle le corps resiste en quelque façon au mouvement; en sorte qu'il faut employer une force pour l'y mettre."Leibnitz, *Oeuvres philosophiques* (Philosophical Works), ed. Janet, 2:520.

25. "Cela fait connaître,qu'il y a dans la matière quelque autre chose, que ce qui purement géometrique, c'est à dire que l'étendue et son changement tout nu. Et à le bien considérer on s'aperçoit, qu'il y faut joindre quelque notion supérieure ou métaphysique, savoir celle de la substance, action et force; et ces notions portent, que tout ce qui pâtit doit agir reciproquement, et que tout ce qui agit doit pâtir quelque réaction. Je demeure d'accord que naturellement tout corps est étendu, et qu'il n'y a point d'étendue sans corps. Il ne faut pas néanmoins confondre les notions du lieu, de l'espace ou de l'étendue toute pure, avec la notion de la substance, qui outre l'étendue renferme la résistance, c'est-à-dire l'action et la passion." Ibid., p. 521.

26. Ibid., p. 524.

27. Ibid., p. 525.

28. Ibid., p. 526.

29. Ibid., pp. 527, 528.

30. The *principium indentatis indiscernibilium* states that entities *all of whose features* are identical make up a single entity, so that all actual entities have certain distinctive features.

31. Leibniz, *Oeuvres philosophiques*, 2:595, 596.

32. Solovyov's Russian version, based on *Principien der menschlichen Erkenntniss* (trans. Ueberweg, p. 22) diverges significantly from Berkeley's original. Here is the original text: "That neither our thoughts, nor our passions, nor ideas formed by the imagination, exist without the mind is what everybody will allow. And to me it seems no less evident that the various sensations or ideas imprinted on the Sense, however blended or combined together (that is, whatever objects they compose), cannot exist otherwise than in a mind perceiving them. I think an intuitive knowledge may be obtained of this, by any one that shall attend to what is meant by the term *exist* when applied to sensible things. The table I write on I say exists; that is, I see and feel it: and if I were out of my

study I should say it existed; meaning thereby that if I was in my study I might perceive it, or that some other spirit actually does perceive it. There was an odour, that is, it was smelt; there was a sound, that is, it was heard; a colour or figure, and it was perceived by sight and touch. This is all that I can understand by these and the like expressions. For as to what is said of the *absolute* existence of unthinking things, without any relation to their being perceived, that is to me perfectly unintelligible. Their *esse* is *percipi*; nor is it possible that they should have any existence out of the minds or thinking things which perceive them." [From *Of the Principles of Human Knowledge,* 3.]—Trans.

33. *Principien der menschlichen Erkenntniss,* trans. Ueberweg, 33–36.

34. Ibid., pp. 100–101.

35. Ibid., p. 55.

36. David Hume. *Untersuchung uber den menschlichen Verstand,* trans. Kirchmann, pp.18–19.

37. Ibid., p. 24.

38. The word "thing" (*Ding*) is used here by Kant in the sense of an object in general, without any determination, in the sense of "something," *quelque chose.*

39. "Ich bin der Gott der Welt, den sie im Busen hegt,
     Der Geist, der sich in der Natur bewegt."
     (Goethe's *Faust,* Part 1).

40. Only the general basis of Hegel's system is expounded here. A more detailed exposition (especially of the point of departure and method) of this system, and a very substantial critique of it, can be found in N. G-v's articles in *Russkaya Beseda,* 1859, vol 3. Besides this remarkable work, a just, though too general, critique of philosophical rationalism can be found in certain articles of Khomyakov and I. Kireevsky. [N. G-v is probably Nikita P. Gilyarov-Platonov—Trans.]

41. As is well known, this serves as the basis of Anselm's ontological proof of God's existence, as modified by Descartes.

42. Kant admits the possibility that these two inner essences are *one and the same,* differing only in manifestation or representation.

43. The matter of our knowledge is constituted by sensations, but they themselves are completely empty, so that all *determinate* content is given by the forms of our knowledge. That is, content is only ideal (in the sense of subjective), and, therefore, no actual, independent content can be found in our knowledge.

44. If my memory does not deceive me, Mr. N. G-v, in the aforementioned article, explains this connection in the following way. Hegel's principle asserts: Immediate reality has its being (is) *only* in concept, not in itself.

In other words, being = concept. Hence, concept is everything. But if being (immediate reality) is thus absolutely identical with concept, if there is no difference between them, it would make no difference if we were to reverse the equation and say concept = being (i.e., immediate being). And since concept is everything, it follows that immediate being is everything; immediate activity in human beings, however, is their animal nature, the life of instinct, while in the objective world it is external material being; the exclusive acknowledgement of the animal nature in human beings and of external material being in the objective world is precisely materialism. This argument, in essence completely just, has the form of a sophism, and, in any case, it has never entered the head of any materialist. We can indicate a more natural transition from Hegel to materialism—a transition that, probably, was more or less consciously accomplished by the materialists themselves (of course, by those materialists who had some understanding of Hegel's philosophy).

45. This aspect has been expressed in the anthropological philosophy of the clever and talented Feuerbach. However, in defining the human being's essence, Feuerbach arrived at the crudest materialism. Thus, in one of his last works he seriously put forward a bad pun as a principle: "*der Mensch ist was er isst*" (the human being is what he eats).

46. A translation back from the Russian.—Trans. The Russian is from Herbert Spencer's *Sobranie sochinenii* (Collected Works), ed. Tiblen, Installment 7, p. 106.

47. However, by the necessary limitedness of their principle, they, like the materialists, go to an extreme and deny that logical philosophy has any significance at all. However, the representatives of philosophy, as is perfectly natural, do not have a clear understanding of German philosophy.

48. But in what else can that which truly is be known if not in its manifestation, and what is a manifestation if not an expression of what is manifested, i.e., of that which truly is?

49. "Natur hat weder Kern
Noch Schale:
Alles ist sie mit einem Male.
Dich prüfe du nur allermeist
Ob du Kern oder Schale seyst."
[From Goethe's poem: "On the Contrary (To the Physicist)"].

50. Literally, this sentence reads: "Here everything is actuality [Russian *deistvitel'nost'*; cf. German *Wirklichkeit*], for there is no reality [Russian *real'nost'*; cf. German *Realität*]." Since "actuality" is not a common word in English, I have generally rendered both *deistvitel'nost'* and *real'nost'* as "reality." However, in a few cases (usually when the two terms occur in the same passage or when it is a question of actuality versus potentiality), I have rendered *deistvitel'nost'* as "actuality."—Trans.

51. Spencer, p. 71.

52. Ibid., p., 72.

53. Schopenhauer uses the word *Verstand* not in the sense of the capacity for abstract thinking but in the sense of a capacity for immediate, intuitive (*anschaulich*) representation. He attributes abstract thinking to reason (*Vernunft*). He attempts to prove in detail the correctness of this unusual terminology (in the book *Über die vierfache Wurzel des Satzes vom zureichenden Grunde* [On the Fourfold Root of the Law of Sufficient Ground]), and, as regards the German language, he appears to be right. In Russian the term "*vozzritel'nyi rassudok*" [intuitive rationality] is a *contradictio in adjecto*, but I cannot find a better translation for "*Verstand*" than "*rassudok.*"

54. "Gesetz der Kausalität oder Satz vom zureichendem Grunde des Werdens."

55. "Satz vom zureichenden Grunde des Seyns."

56. "Durch und durch nichts als Kausalität." *Die Welt als Wille und Vorstellung* [The World as Will and Representation], vol.1, p. 10.

57. It is well known that, according to the laws of optics, an object is reflected on the retina in a position inverse to that in which we actually see it. This has always been a stumbling block for physicists.

58. Schopenhauer considers the reverse deduction just as absurd, i.e., the object from the subject as that which knows, for if the object as such is only that which is represented by the subject, in the same way, the subject as such is only that which represents the object and does not exist without representation.

59. "Satz vom zureichenden Grunde des Erkennens."

60. Schopenhauer: *Über die vierfache Wurzel des Satzes vom zureichenden Grunde,* 3d ed., p. 105.

61. "To gignomenon men kai apollumenon, ontōs de oudepote on" (*The Laws*, 891 e).

62. *Die Welt als Wille und Vorstellung*, 3d ed., vol. 1, p. 119.

63. In the same way, all actions upon the body from other objects are immediately felt in the internal consciousness as affects of will—pain or pleasure. Evidently, all so-called internal sensations or affects are only different states of volition. In particular, this was shown by Spinoza in the second and third books of his *Ethica*.

64. Not absolutely immediately, for the form of internal sensation, i.e., time, is preserved. But time alone, without space and causality which condition objective intuition, is an indifferent form, which does not produce any significant change in that which is perceived.

65. *Die Welt als Wille und Vorstellung*, vol. 2, p. 219.

66. Ibid., vol. 1, pp. 126–28.

67. Ibid., vol. 1, p. 345.

68. *Über den Willen in der Natur* (On Will in Nature), 2d ed., 1854, pp. 85-87.

69. Cf. Schopenhauer, *Zwei Grundprobleme der Ethik* (Two Fundamental Problems of Ethics), 2d ed., 1860.

70. *Die Welt als Wille und Vorstellung*, vol. 1, pp. 447–49.

71. Ibid., vol. 1, pp. 485–87.

72. As in Schopenhauer the self-assertive will.

73. "Opektikon de ouk aneu phantasias."—(*On the Soul*, 433 b 29).

74. E. v. Hartmann, *Philosophie des Unbewussten* (Philosophy of the Unconscious), 2d ed., 1870, pp. 90–92.

75. Ibid., p. 3.

76. That is to say, the will and representation of separate individuals.

77. *Philosophie des Unbewussten*, p. 327.

78. In the original: *erkrankt nicht*.

79. In the original: *ermüdet nicht*.

80. *Philosophie des Unbewussten*, pp. 335–42.

81. Ibid., pp. 474, 477, 539.

82. Aristotle, *Metaphysics*. IV:4.

83. In the present chapter I use the words *rassudok* [reason] and *rassudochnyi* [rational] in the generally accepted sense, not in Schopenhauer's sense.

84. This is complacent limitation, opposite to pure reflection or negative reason, into which it thus necessarily passes.

85. Absolute negation of reality in a given sphere is called pure reflection. When abstract reason affirms something that only has particular or abstract truth as an absolute or total truth, and when this noncorrespondence is disclosed by negative reason or reflection, then the negation must necessarily be as absolute as the affirmation was. Thus, for example, when some particular belief or limited form of belief affirms itself as exclusively true, then the negation of this form necessarily becomes the negation of all belief, for the negating reflection can take that which is negated only as that which it gives itself out to be.

86. Further on, we shall have to point out the important positive significance of scholasticism in the development of thought. But in the

meantime we consider it, as we do all of Western philosophy, only in its negative aspect.

87. "The whole essence of these agitated concepts consists in their being opposites in themselves, and of their having peace only in the whole." Hegel, *Werke* (Works), 2d ed., p. 557.

88. Or, in Hartmann's terminology, taken by him from Schelling's "positive philosophy," this (real) principle posits that (*quod*) something is (*dass etwas ist*), whereas the ideal or logical principle determines what (*quid*) it is (*was es ist*).

89. In Schopenhauer the world of forms or the world of representation is pure accident, *accidens*, for the will.

90. "Der Wille als Ding an sich ist das absolut Grundlose."

91. Cf. *Welt als Wille und Vorstellung*, 3d ed., vol. 1, p.179; vol. 2, p.220. *Über den Willen in der Natur*, 2d ed., pp. 46 ff., 63-72.

92. *Hamlet*, Act 3, Scene 1, lines 62–63.

93. "Estin ara anagkēs to mē on epi te kinēseōs einai kai kata panta ta genē kata panta gar hē thaterou psusis heteron apergazomenē tou ontos hekaston ouk on poiei, kai sympanta dē kata tauta outōs ouk onta orth⁻ os eroumen, kai palin, hoti metechei tou ontos, einai te kai onta . . . hopot an to mē on legōmen ouk enantion ti legomen tou ontos, all' het- eron monon." (*The Sophist*, 256e, 257b)—*Platonis opera ex recens*. C.F. Hermanni, 1:402.

94. That is to say, a philosophy which, transcending common possibilities, knows that which actually is, and, also, gives supreme principles for life.

95. Hegel's *Werke*, 2d ed., vol. 3, pp. 32–33.

96. Ibid., p. 47.

97. Ibid., p. 51.

98. Ibid., pp. 38–39.

99. Ibid., p. 87.

100. Ibid., p. 93.

101. Ibid., p. 87.

102. Logical necessity is always conditional. Its general formula is as follows: *If* something exists, then it must satisfy logical laws.

103. Feuerbach, *Das Wesen des Christenthums* (The Essence of Christianity), 2d ed., p. 402.

104. Max Stirner, *Der Einzige und sein Eigenthum* (The Ego and His Own), p. 214.

105. Ibid., pp. 228-29.

106. Ibid., p. 233.

107. Ibid., p. 8.

108. Ibid., p. 248.

109. Ibid., 275.

110. The source of this poem is unknown.—Trans.

111. "Ihr folget falscher Spur!
    Denkt nicht wir scherzen—
    Ist nicht der Kern der Natur
    Menschen im Herzen?"
    (From Goethe's poem "Ultimatum").

112. More precise than the generally used terms "dialectics" and "logic" is the artificial term "gnoseology."

113. Hartmann is so conscientious that those absurdities of his metaphysics which were pointed out by us in their place are by no means given out by him as indisputable truth. See, for example, *Philosophie des Unbewussten*, 2d ed., p. 683. He ascribes a positive significance only to those conclusions of his which, in fact, undoubtedly have such a significance.

114. Since this deism, based on unconscious metaphysics, is sometimes adorned with the generic name "rationalism," it is necessary to call it *vulgar* rationalism in contrast to true philosophical rationalism.

115. So as not to return to this subject, I will say a few words here about materialism. In the development of Western philosophy this system has occupied its proper place at the beginning of modern times, when its best representatives (Hobbes, Gassendi, and others) were active. As an unconscious metaphysics of empiricism, however, this system was professed in the entire subsequent period by empiricists whose thought did not penetrate into the essence of their principle and who were deprived of a philosophical education. In times of intellectual crisis, when true philosophy grows scarce, such unconsciously metaphysicizing empiricists raise their voices and play the dominant role, in the same way that "Wolves are masters in a deserted village." It is just recently that we have seen such a reign of wolves in philosophy.

116. Because the only being that is accessible to us is our own. Consequently, only in this being can we know the other.

117. This term was introduced by Hartmann as the most correct one in the fifth edition of *Philosophie des Unbewusste*, in the chapter: "Das Unbewusste und der Gott des Theismus" (The Unconscious and the God of Theism).

118. "Das Alles umfassende Individuum, welches Alles seyende ist, das absolute Individuum, oder das Individuum katexochēn." *Philosophie des Unbewusste*, 2d ed., p. 474.

119. Schopenhauer's doctrine of eternal ideas, taken entirely from Plato and the Neoplatonists, should not be taken into account, because nowhere does Schopenhauer satisfactorily explain the possible relation of these ideas to metaphysical will, on the one hand, and to subjective representation, on the other. Wherever he speaks about this, he either uses meaningless metaphors or enters into a crude, irreconcilable contradiction with the fundamental principle of his philosophy.

120. As a contemporary representative of such a view one can mention William Hartpole Lecky in his *History of European Morals*.

121. Although its simplicity and primacy can be doubted.

122. It was already shown in the previous chapter that this morality of "general welfare" negates itself and passes into the exclusive arbitrariness of the separate *I*.

123. "Apokatastasis tōn pantōn." (See Acts. 3:21)—Trans.

124. "Synapseias oula kai o uchi oula, sumpseromenon diapheromenon, sunaidon diaidon kai ek pantōn en kai ex enos panta." (Heraclitus)

Notes to Appendix

1. Auguste Comte, *Cours de philosophie positive*, 1st ed., vol. 1, pp. 47–49.

2. Ibid., pp. 2–4.

3. Ibid., pp. 4–5.

4. Ibid., pp. 14–15.

5. For positivism, according to its principle, no sciences exist except natural ones, i.e., those which study phenomena of the external world. Comte does not recognize logic and psychology; he ascribes intellectual and moral phenomena exclusively to the physiology of the nervous system under the name "intellectual and moral functions of the *brain*." Likewise, the science of human society is, for positivism, an external or natural science, since it investigates social phenomena in their external relationships of coexistence and succession. That is why Comte calls this science "social physics," considering its establishment as his most important task, as the culmination of positive sciences in an integral system of *all* positive knowledge.

6. That *théologie* and *état théologique* must signify, for the positivists, *religion in general* is already clear from the fact that the phases of this theological state are *fetishism*, *polytheism*, and *monotheism*. As regards their *métaphysique*, according to the sense of the law it must signify any view that has neither a religious nor a natural-scientific character, i.e., anything that is usually called philosophy—any philosophy with the exception of positivism itself.

7.   "All that does not finally reduce," says Comte, "to some fact observed by means of the senses does not have any reality." It must be noted that Comte recognizes only external observation; he considers internal observation (introspection) to be an absurdity.

8.   Comte, p. 4.

9.   Ibid., pp. 8–9.

10.   In this appendix I use the terms "metaphysical philosophy," "philosophy of metaphysics," and "speculative philosophy" synonymously to refer to all philosophy except positivism. Although not every speculative philosophy is therefore a metaphysical philosophy (for example, Hegel's speculative philosophy even rejects all metaphysics), nonetheless with respect to positivism this distinction has no significance.

11.   Back translation from the Russian.—Trans. This passage from Mill as well as all those that follow are taken from the Russian edition of Lewis and Mill's book *Auguste Comte and Positive Philosophy*.

12.   "Opium facit dormire, quare est in eo virtus dormitiva, cujs est natura sensus assoupire."

13.   Comte, p. 19.

14.   Ibid., pp. 6–7.

15.   The improbable extent of this lack of understanding can be seen in the following argument, placed in the main organ of positivism (*La philosophie positive*, a journal edited by E. Littré et G. Wyrouboff, 1871, No. 3, p. 366): "Il est un mode d'expliquer l'univers, qui soutient que l'homme a été en communication avec Dieu et y est encore sous une forme modifiée. *Eh bien! nous sommons de montrer quoi que ce soit de pratique obtenu de cette façon. Ce n'est certainement pas par de prières que le telegraphe atlantique a été posé, ou le chemin de fer du Pacifique construit.* Il est un autre mode qui prétend, que l'homme porte avec lui en tous temps *une machine (l'esprit)* capable de l'eclairer de la connaissance absolue, de l'instuire de la nature des choses, etc.... Pourtant ce n'est pas là que nous nous sommes adresses *pour recevoir nos oracles par rapport aux moyens convenables d'établir ce cable ou cette voie; ce n'est pas là non plus que vont les astronomes pour apprendre les distance de étoiles ni les chimico-astronomes pour en rechercher les éléments.* D'anciennes traditions parées du nom de révélations, mais pleines de contradictions et d'ignorance notoire et la moderne introspection, riche en prétentions et en découvertes hautement vantées, mais vide de résultats, sont, à la verité, plus autorisées à être appelées religions qu'n'en a la science avec sa méthode homogène, ses résultats qui se verifient l'un l'autre et son immense importance pratique. Mais on trouvera que la science peut plus pour satisfaire toutes les aspirations de l'esprit humain dans l'Europe occidentale et dans l'Amérique, que les assertions des théologiens et les rêveries des introspectionnistes, vainement sanctifiées par l'âge et

couvertes de grands mots. Si ce ne'est pas la l'object de la religion—quel est il?" ["It is a mode of explaining the world which asserts that human beings had been in communication with God and still are so in a modified form. And so! *We demand that this doctrine show that anything at all practical was achieved in that fashion. It was certainly not by prayers that the transatlantic telegraph was laid, or that the Pacific railroad was built.* There is another mode that insists on the fact that human beings always carry with themselves a machine (the mind) that is capable of illuminating them with absolute knowledge, of teaching them the nature of things, etc. However, it is not to it that we address ourselves *to receive our oracles with regard to the most appropriate means for laying this cable or that road; nor do the astronomers turn to it to learn the distances of the stars, nor do the chemical astronomers turn to it to study the composition of the stars.* Ancient traditions, adorned with the words of revelations but full of contradictions and obvious ignorance, and modern introspection, rich in pretensions and in trumpeted discoveries but poor in results, can, to tell the truth, more justly be called religions than science with its homogeneous method, its results that verify one another, and its immense practical importance. But one will find that science can do more to satisfy all the aspirations of the human mind in Western Europe and in America than the assertions of theologians and the reveries of the introspectionists, vainly sanctified by the age and covered with grand words. If this is not the object of religion—what is?"—Trans.] Of course, the best representatives of positivism do not write so stupidly and so ungrammatically. But even if they do not take their lack of understanding to the point of such a caricature, their views essentially differ little from those of this unknown philosopher.

Index

ESALEN INSTITUTE / LINDISFARNE PRESS
LIBRARY OF RUSSIAN PHILOSOPHY

Though it only began to flourish in the nineteenth century, Russian philosophy has deep roots going back to the acceptance of Christianity by the Russian people in 988 and the subsequent translation into church Slavonic of the Greek Fathers. By the fourteenth century, religious writings, such as those of Dionysius the Areopagite and Maximus the Confessor, were available in monasteries. Until the seventeenth century, then, except for some heterodox Jewish and Roman Catholic tendencies, Russian thinking tended to continue the ascetical, theological, and philosophical tradition of Byzantium, but with a Russian emphasis on the world's unity, wholeness, and transfiguration. It was as if a seed were germinating in darkness, for the centuries of Tartar domination and the isolationism of the Moscow state kept Russian thought apart from the onward movement of Western European thinking.

With Peter the Great (1672–1725), in Pushkin's phrase, "a window was cut into Europe." This opened the way to Voltairian freethinking, while the striving to find ever greater depths in religious life continued. Freemasonry established itself in Russia, inaugurating a spiritual stream outside the church. Masons sought a deepening of the inner life, together with ideals of moral development and active love of one's neighbor. They drew on wisdom where they found it and were ecumenical in their sources. Thomas À Kempis's *Imitation of Christ* was translated, as were works by Saint-Martin ("The Unknown Philosopher"), Jacob Boehme, and the pietist Johann Arndt. Russian thinkers, too, became known by name: among others, Grigory Skovoroda (1722–1794), whose biblical interpretation drew upon Neoplatonism, Philo, and the German mystics; N. I.

Novikov (1744–1818), who edited Masonic periodicals and organized libraries; the German I .G. Schwarz (1751–1784), a Rosicrucian follower of Jacob Boehme; and A.N. Radishchev (1749-1802), author of *On Man and His Immortality*.

There followed a period of enthusiasm for German idealism and, with the reaction to this by the Slavophiles Ivan Kireevksy and Alexei Khomyakov, independent philosophical thought in Russia was born. An important and still continuing tradition of creative thinking was initiated, giving rise to a whole galaxy of nineteenth- and twentieth-century philosophers, including Pavel Yurkevitch, Nikolai Fedorov, Vladimir Solovyov, Leo Shestov, the Princes S. and E. Trubetskoy, Pavel Florensky, Sergius Bulgakov, Nikolai Berdyaev, Dmitri Merezhkovsky, Vassili Rozanov, Semon Frank, the personalists, the intuitionists, and many others.

Beginning in the 1840s, a vital tradition of philosophy entered the world stage, a tradition filled with as-yet-unthought-of possibilities and implications not only for Russia herself but for the new multicultural, global reality humanity as a whole is now entering.

Characteristic features of this tradition are: epistemological realism; integral knowledge (knowledge as an organic, all-embracing unity that includes sensuous, intellectual, and mystical intuition); the celebration of integral personality (*tselnaya lichnost*), which is at once mystical, rational, and sensuous; and an emphasis upon the resurrection or transformability of the flesh. In a word, Russian philosophers sought a theory of the world as a whole, including its transformation.

Russian philosophy is simultaneously religious and psychological, ontological and cosmological. Filled with remarkably imaginative thinking about our global future, it joins speculative metaphysics, depth psychology, ethics, aesthetics, mysticism, and science with a profound appreciation of the world's movement toward a greater state. It is *bolshaya*, big, as philosophy should be. It is broad and individualistic, bearing within it many different perspectives—religious, metaphysical, erotic, social, and apocalyptic. Above all, it is universal. The principle of *sobornost* or all-togetherness (human catholicity) is of paramount importance in it. And it is future oriented, expressing a philosophy of history passing into metahistory, the life-of-the-world-to-come in the Kingdom of God.

At present, in both Russia and the West, there is a revival of interest in Russian philosophy, partly in response to the reductionisms implicit in materialism, atheism, analytic philosophy, deconstructionism, and so forth. On May 14, 1988, *Pravda* announced that it would publish the works of Solovyov, Trubetskoy, Semon Frank, Shestov, Florensky, Lossky, Bulgakov, Berdyaev, Alexsandr Bogdanov, Rozanov, and Fedorov. According to the announcement, thirty-five to forty volumes were to be published. This is now taking place.

The Esalen Institute–Lindisfarne Press Library of Russian Philosophy parallels this Russian effort. Since 1980 the Esalen Russian–American Exchange Center has worked to develop innovative approaches to Russian–American cooperation, sponsoring nongovernmental dialog and citizen exchange as a complement to governmental diplomacy. As part of its program, seminars are conducted on economic, political, moral, and religious philosophy. The Exchange Center aims to stimulate philosophic renewal in both the East and West. The Esalen–Lindisfarne Library of Russian Philosophy continues this process, expanding it to a broader American audience.

It is our feeling that these Russian thinkers—and those who even now are following in their footsteps—are world thinkers. Publishing them will not only contribute to our understanding of the Russian people, but will also make a lasting contribution to the multicultural philosophical synthesis required by humanity around the globe as we enter the twenty-first century.